BASIC COMPANION PLANTING

for

SUCCESSFUL VEGETABLE *GARDENING*

A Simplified Beginner's Guide to Using Plant Partners
for Organic Pest Control and Chemical-Free Vegetables

BRUCE MCCORD

For my grandmother Joyce; thank you for sharing your love of gardening with me.

Before you begin, go grab a FREE GIFT!

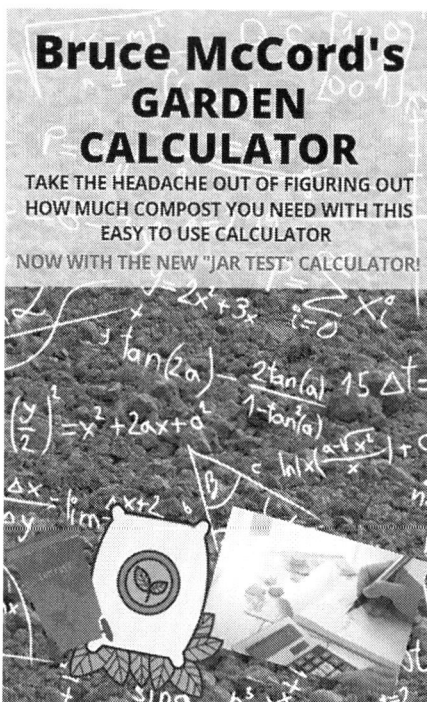

With Bruce McCord's Garden Calculator you will...

- Save time and avoid headaches!

- Save money by avoiding miscalculations

- Easily determine how much compost you need for your garden

- Find out in seconds how many bags, yards, or scoops you need

- Use the same calculator for mulch, topsoil, gravel, virtually ANYTHING

- There's a Metric option too!

Get your FREE COPY today by visiting:
www.BruceMcCord.com

Contents

Introduction

*"A garden is a grand teacher. It teaches patience
and careful watchfulness; it teaches industry
and thrift; above all it teaches entire trust."*
—Gertrude Jekyll, Renowned
British Horticulturist

With nearly 18.3 million new gardeners since the beginning of the COVID-19 pandemic, the world of amateur gardening is exploding in popularity. Many of these budding horticulturists intend to grow vegetables, with one in three households in the United States growing their own food. With the cost of groceries these days, I don't blame them! This is one of the big reasons I got into gardening: I always fantasized about growing all of my vegetables myself. My goal for that first year was to throw a dinner party for all my friends and family, cooking a meal consisting almost entirely of vegetables I grew in my own garden. At the time, this seemed like a perfectly reasonable goal. Oh, how wrong I was!

Unfortunately, high expectations like these often lead to disappointment, and my experience was no different. My first vegetable garden was a complete failure, and I came very close to giving up. I'm very happy I didn't, and through years of trial and error, I can happily say I reached my goal of cooking a dinner comprised entirely from vegetables I had grown.

The truth is, many would-be greenthumbs will strike out on their first attempt in the soil, never to return. Without the right tools and knowledge, it can be very difficult to create a productive greenspace. It's important to be realistic when it comes to amateur gardening, and understand that failing a couple of times is okay! A lot of folks go into gardening thinking it will be very simple, and I understand why. I mean it seems like you just need to put some seeds in the dirt, make sure there's enough sunlight, and throw water on the plants from time to time. But as any experienced greenthumb will tell you, helping a garden flourish isn't as simple as it looks.

Creating a great green space doesn't take days or weeks, but multiple growing seasons over multiple years. Some folks never quite get it right, but I think that comes down to one simple fact: **they never ask for help.** I know I was personally very stubborn at the very start of my gardening career; I too believed that gardening was as easy as it seemed, and just couldn't fathom why all I could seem to grow was a sad patch of weeds. Eventually, I learned to accept the help of others, both in the form of extensive research and speaking to gardeners with more wisdom and experience than myself.

Whether you are completely green or have ample gardening experience, it's never too early to consider companion planting. Like many who discover companion planting, I fell into the practice entirely by accident. I'm constantly striving to create the best possible growing environment for my plants, and in doing so, my gardening methods involve a large amount of experimentation. After placing a basil plant and a tomato plant close together one season (an experience I go into in more detail later), I discovered that a part of my garden that formerly struggled was suddenly flourishing. What had been a constant struggle to find space, fight bugs, and encourage healthy growth became easier almost overnight. So I dove into research mode, and began to learn about this ancient and storied agricultural technique.

The Symbiotic Nature of Companion Planting

A technique dating back thousands of years, companion planting involves placing certain plant types in close proximity, allowing them to benefit from each other's strengths and bolster their weaknesses. Almost every type of plant species you can think of has a companion or group of companions they work best with. Even plants we consider "weeds" can be beneficial, in the right situation. There are also plants that **don't** play nice together; part of proper companion planting is learning which species will hinder the growth of others or attract harmful pests.

If done correctly, companion planting can save you both time and money. The right plants can remove the need for:

- Pesticides
- Herbicides
- Shading implements
- Store-bought fertilizers
- Support structures
- Expensive watering systems

You can beat back bugs, revitalize poor soil, save water, and prevent sunlight damage, while helping increase the individual health and production of your vegetables. Companion plants themselves can often be harvested, adding to the overall yield of your garden. Believe me, some years I have more vegetables than I know what to do with! If your goal is to have as many edible vegetables as possible throughout the growing season, companion planting is just the thing you'll need.

What This Book Will Cover

Each chapter of this book is designed to help you tackle a different aspect of your companion planting journey. We'll start by discussing the history of companion planting itself, traveling back in time to visit different societies ranging from Native American tribes to the ancient Greeks and Romans.

Then, I'll go into some of the common mistakes many people make during their first couple of growing seasons and with companion planting in particular. Picking the right time, spot, soil, and maintenance techniques are all essential to your success, so we'll dive into how to avoid the pitfalls that often create problems for new companion planters.

After that, we'll discuss planning the type and layout of your companion garden, as well as the kind of soil you'll want to use for different plant combinations. This includes studying optimal texture, healthy garden characteristics, and tips to improve subpar soil. A big part of fixing your soil will involve using compost, which we will talk about in detail.

Then it's on to maintenance; we'll cover the right amount of light and water you should provide for your companion plants, as well as the beneficial (and harmful) insects to look for. Learning these good and bad bugs will be essential to successful companion planting: certain plants attract or deter different insects, so you'll want to learn the right species and placement to help bring helpful critters in.

Then it's on to the finale – companion plants and weeds you'll want in your garden. We'll start with weeds, talking about the negative effects and little known benefits many of these species can bring. After that, I'll talk about the best plant combinations I have personally used over the years, showing the "friends" and "enemies" of each species, and going over tips that can help your companion plants thrive.

By the end of this book, you'll have everything you need to start successfully companion planting. I've been gardening for many years now, and the only thing that brings me more joy than a bountiful harvest is helping another gardener find success. I truly believe that, with the right attitude and elbow grease, anyone can create a lush and beautiful green space. Companion planting feels almost like a "cheat code" in that sense: with a bit of know-how, you can vastly improve the number of healthy plants (and subsequent edible vegetables) you can grow in a single season. It took me years to discover and implement this technique; I don't want anyone else to have to struggle the way I did.

So let's dig deep into this fertile subject, and start with answering the first question on many people's minds: **What is companion planting?**

Chapter 1

Greenery Loves Company: A Closer Look at Companion Planting

Did You Know?

Native Americans have long used a technique for companion planting known as "The Three Sisters." Tribes would often plant corn, beans, and squash together in the same area due to the symbiotic relationship that forms between these vegetable types. The beans help boost nitrogen in the soil for the corn and squash, the squash provides shaded, cool soil for the corn and beans, and the corn helps provide support for the beans to grow. The Native Americans had worked out through trial and error that this system really worked, and it still does!

What is Companion Planting?

Our journey to understand companion planting will weave through a variety of topics, but let's start with the absolute basics. The main driving force behind companion planting is the quest for optimal garden growth. Agriculturalists have spent thousands of years trying to find the best ways to make their plants flourish, and with companion planting, they've chosen to seek the help of experts on the subject: other plants!

Companion planting: The close planting of different plants that enhance each other's growth or protect each other from pests.

Basically, through endless trial and error, we've found some plants that not only grow together without interfering with one another, but which actually have an active role in facilitating the growth of their fellow flora. This practice of growing different plants together boosts their growth potential while helping make the most efficient use of the space and water available.

Companion planting has a storied history, having been tinkered with by countless professional agriculturists and amateurs alike. With variations of the practice spanning a diverse array of societies throughout history, companion planting has been changed and improved drastically since its humble beginnings.

How Did Companion Planting Start?

Your uninformed gardener friend will most likely tell you that companion planting started in the 1970s, around the same time the organic movement exploded in popularity. In the '70s, worldwide concern for environmental pollution was reaching a boiling point, with many activist groups citing improper farming techniques as a direct contributor to climate change. So the organic movement was born; environmentally conscious consumers began to choose food that was grown locally using sustainable practices, and gardeners began to adopt these same practices in their backyards. One of the techniques these growers would use to conserve water was, naturally, companion planting. This type of planting lends itself well to the organic movement, offering a way to protect the planet while making gardens more lush and bountiful.

While the organic movement was an excellent idea, and we're still experiencing the benefits of its proponents to this day, it was **not** responsible for the concept of companion planting. No, for that, we'll have to travel a bit further back than the 1970s. In fact, we'll need to turn the clock back thousands of years.

The Ancient Origins of Companion Planting

While there is evidence of companion planting being practiced 10,000 years ago or more, the oldest written records we have of companion planting come from the Greeks and Romans nearly 2,000 years ago, who utilized the practice to help boost the production of their favorite beverage: wine.

A book written in the second century BC by an author named Marcus Terentius Varro describes the practice in detail, recounting stories of witnessing growers placing plants in specific patterns to enhance benefits or avoid conflicts that often occur. Walnut trees and cabbage were common culprits responsible for restricting growth, and Varro noticed that any plants that attempted to grow nearby would struggle immensely.

> *"If he has an oak grove near the boundary,*
> *you cannot well plant olives along such a*
> *forest; for it is so hostile in its nature that*
> *your trees will not only be less productive,*
> *but will actually bend so far away as to lean*
> *windward toward the ground, as the vine is*
> *wont to do when planted near the cabbage."*
> —Marcus Terentius Varro

In a similar fashion, Roman agriculturists noticed that walnut trees prevented their grape vines from flourishing, drastically reducing their yields and subsequent profits. This led to the discovery of a biological process we know now as allelopathy.

> **Allelopathy:** The chemical inhibition of one plant (or another organism) by another due to the release into the environment of substances acting as inhibitors to germination or growth.

As the Romans spread word of this new discovery, growers worldwide began to notice the effects plants had on others nearby. Then, as it seemed that societies across the globe were on the precipice of massive agricultural advancements, the Dark Ages struck. Progress was slowed, and major leaps in companion planting wouldn't happen for hundreds of years.

Post-Dark-Age Planting

Several different societies made contributions to the technique in the centuries that followed. European monks used forms of companion planting in their monasteries. However, living in closed religious communities, these monks only shared their methods with other monasteries. There may have been written records, but in the 16th century, Henry VIII dissolved all monasteries after a disagreement with the Catholic Pope, and many records were lost.

The Chinese also made significant advancements in the field of companion planting 1,000 years ago with their unique use of mosquito ferns. By planting these ferns in a similar way that companion planters would use beans, Chinese farmers found that their rice yields would improve drastically. It turns out that mosquito ferns provided shade and increased nitrogen in much the same way beans would, making them a valuable asset for crops with too much direct sunlight.

The next big move forward took place in the late 17th and early 18th centuries with a man called Jethro Tull. Tull, born in 1674, was an English agriculturist and inventor who, while sitting on a park bench, helped create the foundation for modern British agriculture. (If you got my horrible joke, I like you.) Though he's known for many advancements in the field of agriculture, his most significant contribution to companion planting was his study of the effects of weeds on regular crops. While it's common knowledge now, his work showed just how detrimental certain plants were to one another when grown too close to others.

Another agriculturist named "Turnip" Townsend further helped by creating the four-crop rotation method. This shifting in the position of vegetable growth patterns helped to decrease the number of pests and diseases that blighted crops. It also increased the available nutrients through the use of plants that naturally raised the levels within the soil.

Even Charles Darwin took a small break from creating the theory of evolution to help expand the field of companion planting. By observing growing fields of hay in two different villages, Darwin noticed that one village would plant it closely with red clover. He discovered that the red clover helped create richer soil, producing much larger amounts of harvestable hay. From this, Darwin concluded that the richer an environment is in available nutrients, the better the plants (or animals, for that matter) will grow.

As we continue into the modern era, companion planting is still widely used by amateur and commercial farmers alike. While there is some naysaying when it comes to the practice, many gardeners swear by the technique. With thousands of years of history behind companion planting, how can we disagree?

How Does Companion Planting Work?

While there are a number of different procedures for each plant pairing, the basic idea is to grow two different kinds of plants that benefit one another in close proximity. This can help each plant out in a number of ways, including:

- Better nutrient uptake
- Reduced need for pesticides
- Improved pest management
- Enhanced ability to pollinate
- Shade and temperature regulation
- Much higher yield potential

An excellent example of this in action is pairing different vegetables with beans. You can see from the "Three Sisters" fun fact that beans actually increase the amount of nitrogen in the soil, one of the essential nutrients required for plant growth. This nitrogen creates a more hospitable environment for a number of vegetables, including cabbage, carrots, and beets, allowing them to reach their full potential and yield more bountiful harvests come fall.

The scientific community is a bit stricter when it comes to the term "companion planting," as it refers to a broad set of practices that often rely on informal knowledge. For knowledge of companion planting to be considered scientific, it must be arrived at through controlled plant combination experiments. As a result, these experiments are rarely referenced as "companion planting" tests and are more often called "intercropping," "polyculture," or "plant associations." While these experiments haven't confirmed every technique companion planters use, many of the combinations already known by practitioners have proven effective in clinical trials.

Scientists have found that through intercropping, as they call it, the growth cycle of plants releases all kinds of chemical attractants or repellents, bringing in insects that can help with pollination or repelling bugs that would do your plants harm. A great example of this is the common onion: the odors from an onion help deter insects that would munch on leaves and stems, helping protect any companion plants from damage.

Onions are far from the only plant that can act as a natural pest deterrent. There are numerous examples, but here are ten common species you can plant to make sure those pesky bugs leave your garden alone.

Ten Bug Deterring Plants

1. Petunias
2. Mint
3. Chrysanthemums
4. Basil
5. Lemongrass
6. Lavender
7. Marigold
8. Chives
9. Citronella Grass
10. Rosemary

On the other end of the spectrum, you have plants that actually *attract* insects. While it may seem counterintuitive, some bugs are actually very beneficial for your garden. Let's look at a few of the good insects you want crawling around your soil and which plants you'll need to lure them in. You can refer back to this section later on when deciding on companion plants to use in your garden.

Six Bugs You Want On Your Team

1. Lacewings

Prey: Aphids

What Should I Plant to Attract Them?

- *Carum carvi* — Caraway
- *Coriandrum sativum* — Coriander
- *Achillea* filipendulina — Fern-leaf yarrow
- *Anethum graveolens* — Dill
- *Angelica gigas* — Angelica
- *Anthemis tinctoria* — Golden marguerite
- *Atriplex canescens* — Four-wing saltbush
- *Tanacetum vulgare* — Tansy
- *Callirhoe involucrata* — Purple poppy mallow
- *Cosmos bipinnatus* — Cosmos white sensation
- *Daucus carota* — Queen Anne's lace
- *Foeniculum vulgare* — Fennel
- *Helianthus maximiliani* — Prairie sunflower
- *Taraxacum officinale* — Dandelion

9

2. Tachinid Flies

Prey: Caterpillars, stink bugs, squash bug nymphs, beetles, flies

What Should I Plant to Attract Them?

- *Phacelia tanacetifolia* — Phacelia
- *Tanacetum vulgare* — Tansy
- *Petroselinum crispum* — Parsley
- *Thymus serpyllum coccineus* — Crimson thyme
- *Mentha pulegium* — Pennyroyal
- *Anthemis tinctoria* — Golden marguerite
- *Eriogonum fasciculatum* CA — Buckwheat
- *Melissa officinalis* — Lemon balm

3. Hoverflies

Prey: Aphids and Mealybugs

What Should I Plant to Attract Them?

- *Astrantia major* — Masterwort
- *Atriplex canescens* — Four-wing saltbush
- *Callirhoe involucrata* — Purple poppy mallow
- *Anthemis tinctoria* — Golden marguerite
- *Aster alpinus* — Dwarf alpine aster
- *Achillea millefolium* — Common yarrow
- *Ajuga reptans* — Carpet bugleweed
- *Allium tanguticum* — Lavender globe lily
- *Alyssum saxatilis* — Basket of Gold
- *Anethum graveolens* — Dill
- *Lobularia maritima* — Sweet alyssum — white
- *Melissa officinalis* — Lemon balm
- *Mentha pulegium* — Pennyroyal
- *Mentha spicata* — Spearmint
- *Monarda fistulosa* — Wild bergamot
- *Carum carvi* — Caraway
- *Chrysanthemum parthenium* — Feverfew
- *Coriandrum sativum* — Coriander
- *Cosmos bipinnatus* — Cosmos 'White Sensation'
- *Daucus carota* — Queen Anne's lace
- *Eriogonum fasciculatum* CA — Buckwheat
- *Foeniculum vulgare* — Fennel
- *Lavandula angustifolia* — English lavender
- *Limnanthes douglasii* — Poached egg plant
- *Limonium latifolium* — Statice
- *Linaria vulgaris* — Butter and eggs
- *Lobelia erinus* — Edging lobelia
- *Penstemon strictus* — Rocky Mt. penstemon
- *Petroselinum crispum* — Parsley
- *Achillea* filipendulina — Fern-leaf yarrow

11

4. Parasitic Wasps

Prey: Moths, Butterflies, Beetles

What Should I Plant to Attract Them?

- *Callirhoe involucrata* — Purple poppy mallow
- *Carum carvi* — Caraway
- *Coriandrum sativum* — Coriander
- *Cosmos bipinnatus* — Cosmos white sensation
- *Limonium latifolium* — Statice
- *Linaria vulgaris* — Butter and eggs
- *Lobelia erinus* — Edging lobelia
- *Lobularia maritima* — Sweet alyssum – white
- *Melissa officinalis* — Lemon balm
- *Mentha pulegium* — Pennyroyal
- *Sedum kamtschaticum* — Orange stonecrop
- *Tagetes tenuifolia* — Marigold – 'Lemon Gem'
- *Tanacetum vulgare* — Tansy
- *Thymus serpyllum coccineus* — Crimson thyme
- *Petroselinum crispum* — Parsley
- *Potentilla recta 'warrenii'* — Sulfur cinquefoil
- *Potentilla villosa* — Alpine cinquefoil
- *Allium tanguticum* — Lavender globe lily
- *Anethum graveolens* — Dill
- *Anthemis tinctoria* — Golden marguerite
- *Astrantia major* — Masterwort
- *Achillea filipendulina* — Fern-leaf yarrow
- *Achillea millefolium* — Common yarrow
- *Daucus carota* — Queen Anne's lace
- *Foeniculum vulgare* — Fennel
- *Zinnia elegans* — Zinnia – 'Lilliput'

5. Ladybugs

Prey: Aphids

What Should I Plant to Attract Them?

- *Foeniculum vulgare* — Fennel
- *Helianthus maximiliani* — Prairie sunflower
- *Penstemon strictus* — Rocky Mt. penstemon
- *Potentilla recta 'warrenii'* — Sulfur cinquefoil
- *Achillea filipendulina* — Fern-leaf yarrow
- *Achillea millefolium* — Common yarrow
- *Ajuga reptans* — Carpet bugleweed
- *Alyssum saxatilis* — Basket of gold
- *Asclepias tuberosa* — Butterfly weed
- *Atriplex canescens* — Four-wing saltbush
- *Coriandrum sativum* — Coriander
- *Anethum graveolens* — Dill
- *Anthemis tinctoria* — Golden marguerite
- *Daucus carota* — Queen Anne's lace
- *Eriogonum fasciculatum* — California buckwheat
- *Potentilla villosa* — Alpine cinquefoil
- *Tagetes tenuifolia* — Marigold 'Lemon Gem'
- *Tanacetum vulgare* — Tansy
- *Taraxacum officinale* — Dandelion
- *Veronica spicata* — Spike speedwell
- *Vicia villosa* — Hairy vetch

6. Pirate Bugs

Prey: Chinch Bugs, Thrips, Corn Earworms, White Flies, and Spider Mites

What Should I Plant to Attract Them?

- *Carum carvi* — Caraway
- *Cosmos bipinnatus* — Cosmos 'White Sensation'
- *Foeniculum vulgare* — Fennel
- *Medicago sativa* — Alfalfa
- *Mentha spicata* — Spearmint
- *Solidago virgaurea* — Peter Pan goldenrod
- *Tagetes tenuifolia* — Marigold 'Lemon Gem'

14

What Are the Benefits of Companion Planting?

There are so many benefits to companion planting, it could be a chapter all by itself. But, for now, let's talk about a few of the more notable ways companion planting can help your garden's growth, sustainability, and diversity.

- **Deters Pests:** Many plants excrete chemicals that pests hate, generating almost a "force field" around any vegetables or herbs that surround them. These plants can also emit odors that mask the scent of your vegetables, hiding them from the hungry bugs so they don't have the chance to chow down.

- **Attracts Pollinators and Beneficial Insects:** Attracting good bugs is just as crucial as repelling bad ones, and companion planting can bring the beneficial insects you need to defend your plants against pests. They can also bring in the insects you need to facilitate growth, like bees. There are several plants you can put in your garden to attract pollinators, including basil, bee balm, blanket flower, and borage. And those are only the ones that start with the letter B!

- **Shade Regulation:** While plants need to feed off the sun's power with the help of chlorophyll and carotenoids, too much sun can actually be damaging. Those photon-capturing molecules begin to capture too much energy, overloading the plant and dehydrating the surrounding soil. Luckily, companion planting has your back! Many companion plants can offer shade for your sensitive garden residents, allowing them to stay out of the sun during those intense hours in the middle of the day.

- **Natural Support:** We can all use a helping hand from time to time, and even though plants don't technically have hands, they too occasionally need some assistance. Several companion plants offer their flora brethren a form of organic trellis, a structure that allows plants to "climb" and grow freely. Heading back to our "Three Sisters" factoid, we can see an example of one of the best supporting plants: corn! Many plants, like pole beans, can use corn to physically support their climbing growth patterns, helping increase the overall bean yield come harvest time.

- **Weed Suppression:** If you're like me, you want to use as few chemicals in your garden as possible. It's always a shame to go through all the effort to plant a beautiful organic garden, only to sully it by spraying harsh weed killer down from above. But yet again, companion planting comes in to save the day. Low-lying plants with high density, sometimes called cover crops, can help prevent weeds from getting a foothold. By reducing the available space and blocking out the life-giving sun, cover crops prevent most weed species from surviving or thriving. There are many cover crops to choose from, including mint, mustard, rye, clovers, buckwheat, cowpeas, alfalfa, and certain types of grass. These cover crops can also be beneficial as 'green manures' that can be dug into the soil to add nutrients.

- **Adds Diversity, Saves Space, and Boosts General Garden Health:** Nobody wants only one type of plant in their garden, but there is only so much space in the backyard we can use. Companion planting allows you to diversify your greenery by using the same area for multiple plants; not only will you have more veggies to eat in the fall, your vegetables will be that much healthier. This is because companion planting doesn't only add diversity; it also boosts the general health of your garden. With higher nutrients, fewer pests, and more growth support, it's no wonder so many amateur gardeners swear by this ancient practice.

◗ **Increases Productivity:** The big reason many gardeners grow vegetables is obviously so they can eventually eat them! Reaping a bountiful harvest is one of the most satisfying feelings in the world, and the more productive your crops are, the better you'll feel. A variety of factors combine when you use companion planting that can help increase crop productivity, like the reduction of harmful pests, increase in healthy pollination, better availability of nutrients, and the shade provided by certain species.

◗ **Cuts Out the Need For Chemicals:** Unfortunately, the average gardener will use a variety of chemicals to help protect their plants and increase their growth. While this isn't always a bad thing, these chemicals can be expensive. Also, if you are trying to grow as naturally as possible, the fewer chemicals you can use in your garden, the better. Companion planting has many ways of working around the need for artificial pesticides and weed killers. Planting anti-pest species like mint and rosemary can replace many common pesticides, and cover crops like clover work great in suppressing weeds.

◗ **Improves Aesthetics:** Yes, the harvest is great, but many gardeners also want a lush and beautiful biosphere they can show off to friends and family. Instead of an entire crop of a single vegetable, companion planting encourages the intermingling and co-existence of a diverse array of plant life. You can give your garden a "layered" look, with several tiers of various companion plants existing alongside one another. Also, remember that a lot of companion plants are flowers, not just vegetables. You can end up building a garden space that you will love to show off to your friends.

Chapter Wrap-up: Key Points

🌢 Companion planting is the practice of growing two or more plants in close proximity for the benefit of one, or both, species. It works by learning what attributes certain plants bring to the soil and surrounding life; this is usually due to the excretion of chemicals from the plant, or the way they interact with nutrients in the soil.

🌢 Native American tribes have passed down the methods for centuries, with the first use of companion planting dating back almost 10,000 years. The technique was further studied by many societies throughout history, including the Romans, Greeks, Chinese, and English.

🌢 Companion planting has a number of benefits, including healthier growth, increased crop production, determent of pests, attraction of beneficial insects, and better nutrient availability.

Companion Planting is Rich and Complex, So Let's Dig Deep!

Now you have a bit of an idea of what companion planting is, but don't run to your garden just yet! This technique isn't one to be undertaken hastily, and implementing it incorrectly can waste months of time and thousands of dollars. In our next chapter, we'll talk about the common mistakes first-time companion planters make, and how you can avoid them.

Chapter 2

Sow Wrong: Common Mistakes to Weed from your System

Did You Know?

Everyone loves the vibrant yellow, orange, and red of marigolds, but these flowers have a far more important function than aesthetics. In addition to their natural beauty, marigolds secrete alpha-terthienyl from their roots, which is an organic pest repellent. This makes them a favorite for companion planters, who often pair them with tomatoes, squash, and melon. The important thing to remember with marigolds is to leave their roots intact, even at the end of a season. That's where the pest repellent is produced!

Before we dive into the particulars about companion planting, let's discuss one of the biggest truths about amateur gardening: you are going to mess up. Mistakes happen, and it's completely understandable to run into difficulties during your first few seasons. The key is to learn from these mistakes and seek the wisdom of those who have dealt with them for years. That way you can save the time, money, and effort that can often be wasted on unresponsive or weed-filled patches of dirt.

Ten Gardening Mistakes to Avoid

Whether it's companion planting or regular old gardening, certain issues always seem to pop up when we begin messing around in the soil. I have personally made many of these mistakes myself. In the past, I've chosen the wrong spot for my plants, overexcitedly planted early, neglected my soil, and failed to protect my garden from pests and disease. I say this to let you know that even after you learn about these common traps, you may still fall into them anyway. That being said, knowing as much as you can before planting goes a long way;

with the right know-how, you can avoid many of these failures right from the start and increase your chances of a lush first-time garden.

1. Planting Too Early or Too Late

The early bird gets the worm, but the early gardener might not get any worms (or harvestable crops) at all! We all get antsy during the winter and think, "Well, I can just start growing some of my plants inside. They'll just be that much bigger when I transfer them to my garden!" So you plant too soon before the last frost date, and crowd your home with more pots than that meager light through your windows can support. Before long, you've found yourself with plants that are quickly moving beyond their growing space, reaching out as they struggle to find a reliable source of light.

> **Frost Date:** Average date of the last light freeze in spring or the first light freeze in fall.

Planting too late can also bring a whole heap of trouble to a burgeoning garden. Putting your seeds into soil too late in the year (which, depending on the plant in question, can be any time from July to October) will usually result in poor, or no, germination. Conditions like cold temperatures, excessive moisture, and a lack of proper sunlight create a sub-optimal environment for most seedlings to grow. Even if your plants are specifically bred for cold weather, like kale, spinach, and certain types of lettuce, they will still need a certain minimum temperature to germinate. Anything less than 60 degrees Fahrenheit will be difficult, and anything below 50 degrees will be nearly impossible.

2. **Neglecting to Harvest**

For most, harvesting is the part of gardening they look forward to. But how do you know when your vegetables are ready to harvest? This question overwhelms some amateur gardeners, who fear they will harvest their crops too early out of overexcitement. In their caution, they allow their vegetables to over ripen and rot. Many plants need to be harvested not only once, but multiple times per season. This is especially true with herbs like basil and cilantro, which will branch out and grow fuller with each harvesting. If you see your plant has its branches filled and the veggies are ripe, don't hesitate: harvest away!

3. **Picking the Wrong Spot**

Much like real estate, gardening is all about location, location, location. Take some time to look at the layout of your backyard, deck, or wherever you plan to establish your greenery. Picture your potential garden filled with plants, and ask yourself a couple of questions:

◖ **Will My Plants Have Enough Room?**

Consider the types of plants you intend to grow in this space; will they grow tall enough to brush any overhangs, wide enough to push their way outside the boundaries of your gardening structure, or heavy enough to break anything below them? This is especially important when it comes to companion planting, because you'll have several species growing in close proximity. If there isn't enough room for each plant, they may have difficulty getting enough nutrients, water, and sunlight. Speaking of sunlight...

◖ **Is There Sufficient Sunlight?**

Depending on the type of plant, the residents of your garden could require at least six hours of direct sunlight each day to grow properly.

Without the right amount of sunlight, plants won't be able to produce chlorophyll and will likely turn a sickly yellow or white.

> **Chlorophyll:** A green pigment, present in all green plants and in cyanobacteria, responsible for the absorption of light to provide energy for photosynthesis. Its molecule contains a magnesium atom held in a porphyrin ring.

Without the energy produced via this pigment, your plants will begin to grow upward and stretch their stems in a desperate search for light. This puts tremendous stress on your crops, and will surely hamper your harvest.

How Much Natural Water Will My Plants Get?

While you will have a regular watering schedule for your garden, choosing the right spot means considering how much natural water your plants will receive. This doesn't just refer to what type of climate you live in, or how much rainfall your section of the world gets. When choosing a spot, you have to consider what physical obstacles will prevent your plants from getting enough rain, or shield them from receiving too much. This includes awnings, overhangs, nearby trees, and anything else that could impede raindrops from reaching your plant's roots. Make sure to also have your watering station established near your garden, to make watering that much easier. Just like with sunlight, water is one of the foundational elements all successful gardens are built upon. The more consistent your watering is, the better your plants can grow.

4. **Not Spacing Properly**

While companion planting is all about different plants co-mingling in close cohabitation, you want to make sure they aren't encroaching on each other's growth. Yes, certain vegetables like beets and lettuce can be planted in close proximity and thinned later during harvest. But some plants can start out as tiny seedlings and blossom into weaving networks of vines and branches. Be aware of how close you are placing plants that can block the sun or expand into other crops' root systems. Corn is a common culprit: as it grows into its signature stalks, corn can easily block the sunlight for plants lower to the ground. Plants with large vine systems like squashes or cucumbers can reduce the air circulation for other vegetables, making it difficult for them to get the oxygen they need. Research each potential occupant of your garden carefully, and make sure that the plants around them are friends, not foes.

5. **Skimping on Your Soil**

Just as vital as proper sunlight and adequate water, healthy soil forms the environment within which your plants can thrive. You need to make sure your soil has a good balance of the three primary nutrients:

- **Nitrogen:** Essential for plant function, nitrogen helps form the building blocks for plant proteins and enzymes. These proteins serve as the structural materials with which plants build their organic matter, and facilitate a large number of the biochemical reactions taking place within your garden.

- **Phosphorous:** Phosphorous is one of the building blocks for adenosine triphosphate or ATP, an energy molecule found in all forms of life. ATP helps provide plants with energy through the process of photosynthesis. From seedling to maturity, phosphorus helps maintain a plant's health and give it the fuel it needs to grow as strong as possible.

🌢 **Potassium:** Nutrients need help moving throughout a plant's structure, and potassium helps to facilitate this process. Potassium also helps activate enzymes within a plant, helping further aid the production of ATP. This regulates the rate of photosynthesis and facilitates sustainable growth.

The right soil won't just have nutrients though, and seeds won't be the only life growing in your garden. For plants to thrive, there needs to be a healthy ecosystem of beneficial organisms, the most important of which is earthworms. Earthworms are responsible for so many parts of what makes healthy soil beneficial to plant life, including:

🌢 Nutrient cycling

🌢 Water movement

🌢 Soil aeration

🌢 Infiltration

By helping organic matter decompose, earthworms create the perfect environment for plants to grow. But they can only help if they're in the soil.

Getting your soil perfect is no easy task, but it's essential to successful companion planting. There just isn't enough room in this chapter to discuss every facet of good soil science; you can find that in my previous book, Basic Soil Science for Successful Vegetable Gardening.

6. **Planting Too Much**

We all get overzealous every now and then, especially when we're excited about a new hobby. I was certainly guilty of overplanting in my earlier days, with images in my head of providing delicious veggies to friends and family, or maybe even setting up a little stand at a farmers market. Unfortunately, there is only so much work one gardener can handle, and overplanting often leads to getting sloppy. Having a large green space with a wide variety of different plant species is complicated, and each type of vegetable you grow will need a different level of care and attention. Learning what each plant needs, and accommodating its needs with that of your other crops, can be a daunting task. It's always better to start small for your first few seasons. I promise, as your experience grows, so will your garden!

7. **Forgetting to Stagger Harvest Times**

One of the more effective methods you can use to increase your production is succession planting. Succession planting involves harvesting at different intervals, instead of the "all-at-once" way many first-time gardeners will use. This will allow plants in different stages of growth to utilize the available resources more effectively, and you'll be able to eat the fruits (or vegetables) of your labor at a more leisurely pace. When all of your crops are ready at the same time, you may find some of your hard-earned veggies going to rot.

8. **Putting Off Routine Maintenance**

Just like taking your car in for a regular oil change, there are certain tasks your garden will require on a routine basis in order for it to thrive. There are three primary components to a good maintenance program:

> ◗ **Get Those Pesky Weeds:** While companion planting is all about a variety of flora and fauna cohabitating peacefully,

there is one type of plant that can't exist in harmony: weeds. These obnoxious and invasive species can sap the nutrients from your garden, invite pests, and absorb water intended for your precious plants. You'll need to pull these suckers out of the ground on a regular basis, making sure to get the entire root so they can't grow back. That is, unless you are following hard core 'no dig' methods. In that case, you would just cut the weeds off at the surface. But that's another book.

◗ **Give Your Plants Food:** You'll want to provide your plants with all the compost and fertilizer they need to grow up big and strong; adding a layer of organic material every once in a while can balance nutrient levels and promote higher crop yields.

◗ **Hydrate Your Greenery:** Depending on what type of climate you live in and the species you plant, you'll want to water your plants anywhere from once a day to once every few days. You can also use an automatic watering system, which can be a huge help for busier or more forgetful gardeners.

9. Planting Without a Fence

You aren't the only one who finds your fruits and vegetables delicious: local animals will see your garden as an all-you-can-eat buffet, with all manner of deer, rabbits, groundhogs, chipmunks, and neighbors coming to stuff their faces. Depending on what type of animals you have in your area, it's best to build a fence that can prevent critters from consuming your hard work.

For intruders like deer, you'll need a fence high enough to prevent them from jumping over. For burrowing animals, you'll want a barrier to extend below the ground to prevent them from digging their way in. No one wants to wake up in the morning with their beautiful garden torn to shreds; fencing can prevent this nightmare from happening, saving your crops for the person who deserves them most: you!

10. Ignoring The Signs of Poor Health

It can be difficult to keep an eye on every single plant when you have a big garden, not to mention when your attention is taken up by constant watering, weeding, and feeding. Regular monitoring is essential though, and keeping an eye on the health of each of your plants will not only affect their growth, but the growth of their companions.

There are several signs to look out for when it comes to your plants' health:

- **Pest Infestations:** You may think that a pest infestation will be obvious, with droves of angry looking bugs swarming you and your plants like you're in a classic monster movie. The reality is, you'll need to keep a close eye on the physical integrity of your greenery to catch infestations early. The signs can be subtle, such as small holes or chew marks on leaves, shiny trails of slime, or dark green droppings.

- **Signs of Disease:** Like with pest infestations, plant diseases can be hard to see when they first begin affecting your garden. Your plants may seem fine at first, but then you'll notice that their growth is slowing, their stems have become spindly, and they are developing unsightly spots on their leaves and stems.

- **Wilting and Yellowing:** Plants that have lost their luster and begun to wilt or yellow are likely dehydrated, with their cells collapsing due to lack of proper watering. If you observe your plants regularly, you'll be able to tell the moment they start to wilt or develop that tell-tale yellowish coloring.

Common Errors When Companion Planting

We've covered the overall goofs and gaffs many amateur gardeners make, but what about with companion planting specifically? While it may seem simple, planting several species in close proximity can get dicey. Here are a few of the common errors companion planters make on their first go-around.

Error #1: Three (or More) is a Crowd

Yes, the name of the game in companion planting is using your space as effectively as possible, planting as many species as you can in a small area. But there can always be too much of a good thing, and even if plants are compatible, putting too many in a single area can cause crowding. This prevents each individual species from receiving the oxygen, water, and nutrients they need, leading to competition and stunted growth.

Error #2: Down in Front!

Shade can be a valuable resource in areas with too much direct sunlight, and plants that get too much time with the big orb in the sky can suffer immensely. But when it comes to plants that block the sun from their shorter companions, the trouble comes when that shade is working 24/7. If you have too many taller plants like corn or sunflowers in one area, you may find your crops lower to the ground will suffer.

Error #3: The Root of the Problem

The roots of your crops will vary in their depth and size, falling into one of three categories: shallow-rooted, medium-rooted, or deep-rooted. Having too many of the same depth plants in one area can cause competition, and restrict root growth by overlapping with their closest companions. I'll list a few plants here that have different root depths; you'll want a mixture of these, provided they aren't incompatible with one another (check the chart below!)

Deep-Rooted Plants	Medium-Rooted Plants	Shallow-Rooted Plants
Tomatoes	Beans	Lettuce
Asparagus	Cucumbers	Kale
Parsnips	Turnips	Chard
Winter squash	Summer squash	Onions
Pumpkins	Carrots	Corn
	Peas	Broccoli
	Many flowering perennials	Spinach
		Cabbage
		Most flowering annuals

One of the biggest hurdles to overcome when it comes to companion planting is that it isn't an exact science. Companion planting is about a lot of trial and error, and it takes time to find which plants work together and which don't. Speaking of plants that don't work together…

Incompatible Plants: These Species Aren't Friends

One of the issues many new companion planters face is knowing which plants play nice together, and which are bitter enemies. We'll go into a list of compatible plants extensively in Chapter 8, but for now, I want to show you which garden inhabitants you should never grow together. These are plants I have personally found incompatible over the years, or those I have learned about through my research. As you get more experience with companion planting, you will be able to identify new pairings and make this list your own!

Plant	Mortal Enemies
Asian Greens	Parsley
Corn	Tomatoes, Cabbage family
Cucumber	Sage
Beans	Chive, Leeks, Garlic, Onion, Marigold, Peppers
Cabbage family (Kale, Cauliflower, Broccoli)	Peppers, Squash, Strawberry, Tomatoes
Dill	Carrots, Tomatoes
Garlic, Onions, Chives, and Leeks	Peas, Beans, Sage
Peas	Chives, Onion, Garlic
Peppers	Cabbage family, Beans
Potatoes	Tomatoes
Radishes	Potatoes, Kohlrabi, Turnips
Sage	Cucumber, Onion
Carrots	Dill
Squash	Cabbage family
Strawberry	Cabbage family
Tomatoes	Potatoes, Corn, Dill and Cabbage family

Least Compatible: Cabbage family

While this isn't the consensus, I've personally had the most trouble with the cabbage family. If you plan to have broccoli, cauliflower, or kale in your garden, make sure they aren't around one of the many species they compete with. I don't know what it is, but it seems like they just want to *kale* everything around them! Was that funny? I was trying for a pun here by replacing the word kill with kale. I don't think it worked as well as I had hoped.

Time to Dodge Those Pitfalls and Leap into Companion Planting

Now that you know a few of the common mistakes new gardeners make, it's time to create a plan for your companion garden. In our next chapter, we'll discuss the various decisions you need to make before a single seed goes in the ground, and the best way to optimize your garden to create the strongest growing environment possible. You'll need to consider how your climate will affect your companion plants, what the best location will be for your garden, and what layout you will use to plant your seeds. We'll start with a little story about the first time I tried companion planting, and just how poorly that initial outing went.

Chapter 3

Seeds for Growth: How to Get Started with Companion Planting

TRADITIONAL BED
RAISED BED
PLANT PARTNERS
PEST CONTROL
WATERING

Believe it or not, I first started learning about companion planting completely by accident. During one of my first seasons as a gardener, I got a bit cocky and decided I was going to see just how many vegetables I could grow at once. Admittedly, I didn't quite have the space for my ambitious vision, or the time to really tend to that number of plants. I only had a small section of my backyard available to plant in, but that didn't stop me from putting far too many vegetables in the soil all at once. This alone isn't what sunk my garden; with the right tending and pairing of plants, I could have made it work. In fact, a few species of vegetables did okay, especially for one of my first gardening attempts. What didn't do well were my cabbage and cauliflower.

Now, I knew going in that both of these veggies would cause trouble. Cauliflower is a finicky plant, requiring a specific set of criteria to grow properly, and cabbage is similarly high maintenance; both veggies are members of the *Brassica* genus, meaning they have precise nutrient and soil requirements, on top of needing six hours of direct sunlight per day. But I knew this ahead of time, and made sure that these plants occupied the sunniest part of my garden. I also made sure the soil was perfectly tuned (or what I called perfect in those early days.) For brassicas, this means the soil was loamy and slightly acidic. I even stuck to my watering schedule to a T, something I had struggled with the previous season. I thought I was doing everything right! And yet, neither plant was growing right. Both my cauliflower and my cabbage refused to grow heads, and a constant onslaught of pests assaulted them at all times. I just couldn't understand why.

So I dived into research mode, and lo-and-behold I found that these two plants are actually mortal foes. In my quest to give these plants the right amount of sun, I had put them far too close together. Turns out, both cabbage and cauliflower fight for the same nutrients and moisture; while I was busy tending to the million other vegetables I was attempting to grow, these two species were duking it out in a competition that left both lacking the food they needed to thrive. They also attract the same kind of pests, primarily aphids. If I had been paying closer attention, I would have seen the chomp marks lining my plants' stems where the aphids had drained them of their nutrients. But even with constant care, it would have been an uphill battle. I didn't know it at the time, but I had set myself up for failure the second the seeds were in the soil.

Five Tips to Help You Start Companion Planting

The point of that story is that errors happen, and you shouldn't get frustrated. As time goes on, you'll learn which traps to avoid, and what actions will ensure your plants survival. Here are some tips you can use to get started on your companion planting journey and help take some of the stress out of your first season.

Tip #1: Create Your Game Plan

So, what plants are you excited about growing? Which seeds are you most excited about scattering in your garden? Choosing which species you'll be putting in the ground is a fun and important first step when considering what you'll grow this year. It will also help you decide how to space out your rows, and make it far easier to keep track of what is growing where. You'll also need to identify which plants will go where to avoid any unfortunate incompatibilities. If I had made the right plan beforehand, I could have put plenty of space between my cauliflower and cabbage. This would have prevented the nutrient competition and excess of pests, and it's very possible they could have grown into delicious, harvestable crops.

Tip #2: Consider Your Climate

Knowing what type of environment your plants will thrive best in means understanding your climate zone, also known as your plant hardiness zone. Developed by the United States Department of

Agriculture, plant hardiness zones are 13 areas around the planet defined by a certain range of annual minimum temperatures. Temperature is one of the most important factors that define which plants can grow where, so knowing your hardiness zone is essential to producing harvestable crops.

Some vegetables are hardier than others and can grow in a wide number of zones, while others are forced to remain in very specific areas to survive. While the vast majority of plants will thrive in slightly cooler or warmer weather, you may be trying to plant in a more extreme cold or hot environment. While your options may be a bit more limited, don't fret! Here are some plants that grow well in cold and hot weather.

Cold-Weather Plants

- Sweet onion
- Spinach
- Leeks
- Garlic
- Rhubarb
- Broccoli
- Rutabaga
- Kale
- Kohlrabi
- Cabbage
- Chicory
- Brussels sprouts
- Arugula
- Corn salad
- Radish
- Fava beans
- Austrian winter pea
- Turnips

Hot-Weather Plants

- Sunflowers
- Cactus
- Aloe vera
- Yucca
- Coriander
- Sweet potatoes
- Yard-long beans
- Southern peas
- Green beans

- Melons
- Hot peppers
- Corn
- Cucumbers
- Zucchini squash
- Malabar spinach
- Okra
- Amaranth
- Eggplant

Tip #3: Start Small

It's understandable to get overzealous when we first begin planting, and no one would blame you for initially choosing too many veggies for your garden. We all fantasize about rows and rows of delicious crops we can share with friends and family, but the reality is that, without the right level of experience, it's easy to get overwhelmed.

This is exactly what happened to me, as I explained at the beginning of the chapter. I had planted so many different kinds of vegetables that I was busy juggling the care for each, trying to make sure every part of my garden got an equal amount of attention. Unfortunately, this just isn't possible; a large garden can quickly approach the workload of a full-time job, and things will inevitably fall through the cracks. If I had gone with a more reasonably sized plot, I would have been able to recognize the signs some of my vegetables were struggling. If I saw the dropping leaves and crawling pests that had infected my broccoli and cabbage, I could have dealt with those issues immediately. Instead, the time I did spend on these veggies was completely wasted, and it was entirely due to my overambition.

Each plant in your garden will need a different level of care, with variable amounts of nutrients, water, and sunlight required to help them grow. You'll want to research each species you put in your garden carefully, making notes about what their individual needs are. These notes can help you establish guidelines for how you will tend to each throughout the season, preventing undernourishment, overwatering, or improper amounts of sunlight.

Tip #4: Establish Your Expectations

Just like you should when attempting any new hobby or project, it's best to manage your expectations. Your first attempt at companion planting may be a smashing success, with each pairing you use working together in harmony and producing delicious, edible veggies. But what's more likely is you'll accidentally place two plants a bit too close, place a row of the same family together and be swarmed with pests, or unintentionally block the sun from your lower-lying greenery.

You should be forgiving of yourself when it comes to making mistakes early on. The probability of you running into issues is high, and by setting your expectations at a reasonable level, you can more easily manage the stress that can accompany learning a new skill. If your garden doesn't flourish on the first go-around or your companion plants don't quite mesh, don't worry! Take notes, adjust your plan, and be ready to try again next year using the lessons you learned. I promise that eventually your garden will not only meet your expectations, but exceed them.

Tip #5: Jot Down Notes in a Journal

Experimentation is the foundation for good companion planting, and no experiment is complete without diligent note taking. Make separate pages for each type of plant you are growing, and if you feel like getting really in-depth, make a page for each individual plant. You can check in once a week on each veggie, jotting down details about how their growth is progressing, how they are intermingling with nearby plants, whether they are experiencing pest or disease issues, and what outside factors could be affecting their current status.

If there was a lot of rainfall that week, you can note how your plants react to excess moisture. If it was a particularly sunny week, you can mark that down and make sure to water your plants more to compensate. With each change and shift in the environment your plants grow in, you can get closer to identifying what the ideal growing situation is for your garden. Every area is different, and what may work for a gardener an hour away may not work for you. Even if you read all the how-to books in the world and research non-stop, nothing beats real-world exposure and a comprehensive journal of your own experience.

Designing Your Garden Layout

Deciding the layout of your planting plot can make or break the success of your season, and making a plan for your garden should start at the ground level. There are a huge number of ways to design your layout, each with their own set of advantages and disadvantages. There are three main factors that will determine the effectiveness of your layout: **garden type**, **pathway creation**, and **plant position**.

Garden Type

What type of garden you choose will depend on what holds your plants, whether that be a simple plot of dirt or specifically built structures. The design of your garden will help establish a safe environment for your plants, acting as boundaries between your soil and the outside world. There are three primary types of gardens:

1. Traditional Bed

The most standard form of garden, a traditional in-ground bed will involve planting directly into your soil with little actual construction surrounding it. There will be boundaries within which you plant to help you understand where to enrich the soil, but a traditional bed will lack the level of preparation needed for other garden designs.

Advantage: Low Cost

This type of garden doesn't require specialized tools or long construction times, and for the most part can use the soil already present in your backyard. You'll need to enrich the soil by composting, but even this can cost you next to nothing if you use proper recycling methods.

Disadvantage: Open to the Elements

Your plants will be far less protected with this style of garden than almost any other. There is little standing in the way of your plants being blown around by wind, dumped on by rain, or being ravaged by animals. You'll also have a tough time with drainage if heavy rainfall is common in your area; unlike with a raised or container garden, in-ground gardens soak up excess moisture with little way to disperse it.

2. Raised Bed

A raised bed garden involves building a box or other structure to place your soil and plants within, usually made of wood, stone, cinder blocks, or safe plastic. These beds can be as high as you want, ranging from a few inches tall to waist height, allowing you to conveniently tend to plants without stooping over or crouching. You can build several raised beds in a single garden if you want to keep certain plants separated, which can be especially helpful when companion planting.

Advantage: Better Protection from Pests

While a traditional in-ground garden lacks any concrete way to keep out animals and pests, a raised bed garden can put your plants out of harm's way by making them more difficult to reach. Yes, certain critters may still make their way within the walls of your raised bed, but you can be sure that the overall pest population will be much lower. Raised beds also give the ability to put pest deterrents along the walls of your structure, further reducing the number of antagonists your garden has to deal with.

Disadvantage: Can Make Your Plants Extra Thirsty

If you live in an area without significant rainfall, a raised bed garden may not be the best idea. Raised beds have naturally higher drainage, which can be advantageous for those living in an area that experiences a lot of moisture. If your area doesn't, you may find that you'll have to water far more often to keep your plants from drying out. This can be difficult with the many other tasks that gardening requires, and you can quickly find yourself falling behind.

3. Container

A container garden involves the use of several pots, planter boxes, or tubs that serve as the housing for your soil. This gives your plants far more mobility, allowing you to move them around if they need more natural water or sunlight. Depending on the size of your containers you can also separate plants more efficiently, allowing you to keep incompatible plants away from each other.

Advantage: Allows You to Build a Garden with Limited Space

Everyone deserves to have a garden, and containers allow you to plant almost anywhere. Not everyone has access to a backyard, but with containers you can plant in much smaller spaces, like the deck of an apartment. Because plants are so mobile in containers, you can even rotate them in and out of your available outdoor area, letting each get the natural sunlight and water they need.

Disadvantage: More Difficult for Companion Planting

Unless you have very large containers, planting pairs of symbiotic species may be far more difficult with a container garden. There is only so much room in each pot, and even if two plants work well together, you are unlikely to have the proper spacing available to put them in the same container. If confined to a small space, plants will almost always fight for resources, like water. Drying out can be bad in raised beds, but it's even worse in containers. This competition can cause your plants to grow at a slower pace and produce less when harvest time arrives.

Pathway Creation

You'll need free range of motion to move throughout your garden, and properly plotting your pathways will allow you to do so without damaging plants or compacting your soil. There are several ways you can approach your pathway design, starting with creating an outline. This can be done either by drawing a rough approximation of your garden space, or if you have the means, taking an aerial photo. You can do this with a drone, or by standing on a high spot like an upstairs window. You'll use this photo to manually draw paths, making sure to account for automatic watering systems or a hose.

You'll need to choose a good material for your paths as well. I recommend shredded tree bark, a great organic material that won't harm your plants once it begins to break down. You can also choose more solid pathway materials like stone or brick, though these can often be a bit more expensive. If you intend to have plants that create significant shade, small lights may be helpful as well. This can not only make it easier to tend to your lower-lying veggies, but allows you to light up your garden at night for a great aesthetic look.

Plant Position

Once you have your pathways planned, you'll want to use that same sketch to pick out where you'll put your plants. Make notes of what areas receive the most sunlight and rain, so you'll know where to put plants that require more time in the sun and frequent watering. Your plant positions are also incredibly important when it comes to companion planting, as it will give you the framework for which companions will go where. You can find a list of compatible plants in Chapter 8. By choosing the pairs that work the best and placing them close together, you can get the maximum benefit out of each.

The exact way you place your plants will depend heavily on what subtype of layout you choose. There are many ways companion planters have found to structure their garden; which type you choose depends on what species you want to grow, and what your specific goals are as a gardener.

Companion Planting Layout Examples

There is no limit to the ways you can arrange the different planting areas of your garden, with many being conducive to the implementation of companion planting methods. What layout you choose, and what plants you include, depend entirely on your individual goals as a gardener. Here are some of the most common layouts to help get you started.

Traditional Row Gardening Layout

Used in agriculture for thousands of years, this method of traditional gardening involves parallel rows lined up next to each other, each containing one type of plant. This is great for allowing both water and sunlight to reach your entire garden, while also allowing for easy movement between each plant for tending.

For companion planting, this method can be a bit of a struggle due to the uniformity of each row. The usual method with this garden layout is to plant each species together in a row; this is meant to be more efficient, as whatever specific care each type of plant requires can be metered out in a more structured manner. With companion planting, this can actually be detrimental, as you'll often be mixing the types of plants you have in close proximity (referred to as polyculture, which we'll talk about more below.)

Square-Foot Gardening Layout

For those with a more restricted space, a square-foot garden can help you use the available area more effectively by sticking to a series of square plots. Each plot of your garden will be a raised bed, usually eight separate beds with 4x4ft dimensions. You can also use this layout with fewer beds if you don't want to be overwhelmed by dealing with eight separate patches of soil. By arranging your raised beds in a horseshoe shape, you can access each from the gap in the center. If your space is big enough, this center horseshoe can also hold your compost area, allowing you to easily transfer your organic materials to the soil once they are ready.

Perennial Polyculture Garden Layout

While many gardeners don't mind the temporary lifespan of annual plants, perennial plants are far hardier and will return again in the spring.

> **Annuals:** Plants that germinate, flower, seed, and die all within the span of one season.
>
> **Hardy Perennials:** Plants that do not need to be replanted each year, withstanding the cold of winter and blooming in spring, summer, or fall.

Many types of perennial herbs and vegetables thrive in raised beds, benefiting from the enhanced protection and drainage. This style also uses a polyculture design, which means each plot is a mixture of different plant species; obviously this makes it very advantageous for companion planters.

Keyhole Bed Layout

A specialized form of raised bed garden, a keyhole bed is a semi-circular, almost Pac-Man shaped structure that helps separate plants into neatly divided areas. In the center of the bed is a composting area, with a notch to allow for additional organic materials and watering. This makes for a highly fertile soil, while helping disperse water evenly and efficiently. While this method can be a bit limiting for planting multiple species in the same area, it often leads to much higher production.

Organic Form Garden Layout

Likely the least structured layout on the list, the organic form garden involves a mixture of circles and spirals moving in whichever way you see fit. There should be almost no straight lines in an organic garden, because that style of plant growth rarely happens in nature. By emulating the flow of a forest, many gardeners feel this style helps them feel more in tune with their garden. The lack of rigid separation works pretty well for companion planting too!

Mandala Garden Layout

If you're feeling artistic, a mandala-style garden can be a gorgeous way to utilize your available gardening space. It involves planting in concentric circles radiating out from a central point, with pathways laid in between each circle. This method can be a bit confusing for new gardeners, who would probably benefit from a simpler technique like the square-foot layout. But if you want to try something a bit out of the ordinary, a mandala garden could be just the thing you want.

Time to Dig Deep and Get Subterranean

While choosing the general design and layout of your companion garden is important, its significance pales in comparison to the absolute king of garden growth: soil. Getting your soil just right is paramount to bountiful production, and involves more than a little trial and error. In our next chapter, we'll look at the different types of soil, what type will work best for you, and how you can supercharge your garden with the right compost.

Chapter 4

Digging Deeper: It's Soil that Matters

Five Fun Facts About Soil

- For a single inch of topsoil to form, the process of erosion needs to take place for a minimum of **500 years.**

- There are an estimated **70,000 different types of soil** present in the United States.

- If you put just one tablespoon of soil under a microscope and somehow count each organism within, you could see it contains more organisms **than the total human population of the earth.**

- The top layer of the earth actually stores carbon dioxide emissions, and **ten percent of all the CO2 emissions** on the planet are stored in the soil.

- If you analyzed one gram of soil, you would likely find **at least 5,000 different kinds of bacteria.**

Without soil, agriculture would not exist. Soil is the foundation for plant growth, providing the nutrients and environment that allows all plant species to thrive. Therefore, it stands to reason that if your soil is low quality, your garden will be low quality. That's why it's so crucial to choose the right kind of soil for your plants and recognize what healthy soil looks like. By taking the time to get your planting environment in proper working order, you can dramatically increase the volume your garden produces.

Different Types of Soil

There are three primary components of soil: **sand**, **silt**, and **clay**. Each soil type has its own set of advantages and disadvantages, with different plants thriving in specific garden environments.

Sand

You've probably seen this grainy, rough material a thousand times, and you may be thinking "Well that's not soil. I don't exactly see plants growing at the beach!" I completely understand, and while there are plants that grow in very sandy areas, like palm trees, most good soil consists only of a small portion of sand. That being said, sand is still essential to a healthy soil mix: it helps soil drain, preventing plants from becoming saturated with moisture. Too much sand can be an issue though, as it will allow nutrients to wash away too readily.

Silt

In the middle of the moisture spectrum lies silt, which falls directly in between sand and clay. It is rich with minerals like quartz, and tends to have a soap-like, smooth texture. Often confused with sand, silt holds on to water far better and contains a wider array of nutrients. Silt can provide a great growing environment for certain types of plants, particularly those that need a lot more water.

Clay

Often giving off a reddish or brown color due to its iron oxide content, clay has the smallest individual particle size of the three main soil components. Clay has difficulties with drainage, and can be easily compacted when wet. Soils with a high clay percentage can be a bit hard to work with, but having zero clay can reduce the amount of nutrients your soil holds on to.

What Type of Soil Works Best for Vegetable Gardens?

While it depends on the specific kinds of vegetables you hope to grow, the best soil tends to be a mixture of all three components. Areas with large amounts of rain will want to have soil that drains well, while more arid regions need a soil mixture that retains moisture so nutrients aren't washed away. Certain garden types will also want to utilize specific soil ratios; for example, a raised bed garden should have a 50/50 ratio of topsoil and compost, while a traditional garden in clay-heavy soil may need to be amended with shale, vermiculite, and gypsum. Again, the types of vegetables you grow will help guide what adjustments you should make. There are certain characteristics that all healthy soil should have, and it's always good to try to include as many of these beneficial soil elements as possible.

Characteristics of Healthy Soil

While there are a large number of tiny details that make up what we consider "healthy soil", let's take a look at three important characteristics your soil should have.

1. Rich in Organic Matter

Decomposing organic matter is one of the main engines fueling the nutrient richness of your soil. As dead plant material decomposes, it turns into humus.

> **Humus:** The organic component of soil, formed by the decomposition of leaves and other plant material by soil microorganisms.

Humus creates a better texture for your soil, increasing aeration and moisture absorption. This absorption doesn't only help with keeping your plants hydrated; humus also absorbs nutrients, with microorganisms breaking down the matter and allowing your plants to take up the goodness.

2. The Right Texture

Many gardeners believe the best type of topsoil is loam, which is a mix of 40% sand, 40% silt, and 20% clay. Loam is very conducive to growing, though some of your plants may prefer a different type of environment. A good loam will be loose and crumbly, meaning that there is a good balance of oxygen and water within its particles. This helps improve root growth and prevent plants from being compacted.

3. A Good pH Balance

Your soil's pH will determine how acidic your garden is, which can be a huge factor in mineral availability. Your plants need minerals to grow big and strong, and the closer you can get your pH to neutral, the better environment they will have. This isn't a hard and fast rule: some plants like lower pH, some like it higher. But for the most part, a neutral pH is the best option to shoot for. This will help increase the production of your vegetables and make for a much more plentiful harvest.

If My Soil Isn't Quite Right, How Can I Improve it?

Not everyone's soil will be perfect right away, and getting your growing environment just right will take a bit of tinkering. Luckily, there are plenty of ways you can improve your soil, starting by giving it a close examination through the process of soil testing.

Conduct Soil Tests

Don't worry, we aren't talking about breaking out the chemistry set or trying to find a reputable soil lab. While "soil testing" can sound daunting, there are a couple of simple tests you can conduct at home to see how your soil is doing. There are five I personally swear by, which I'll briefly describe below. I go into each of these in much more detail in my previous book, *Basic Soil Science for Successful Vegetable Gardening*. In that book, I explain in depth how to perform each of these tests. But for now, let's do a quick overview.

1. **The Jar Test:** If you want to find out what ratio of sand, silt, and clay your soil has, the jar test is just what you need. By taking a clear jar or other translucent container, you can take samples from a few places in your garden and mix them together. You'll then add water until the jar is nearly full and mix everything together. Once you put the lid on, you'll shake the jar until you are certain everything has intermingled, then let it sit for 24 hours. As the mixture settles, each part of the soil will form a different layer in your jar. Sand is the heaviest and will settle first, then silt, then clay. You'll then measure what percentage each layer takes up in your jar, and you'll have a rough estimation of your soil's ratio. This QR will take you to a video of me demonstrating the technique.

52

2. **The Earthworm Test:** Earthworms are one of the most important microorganisms, helping to make sure your garden maintains good levels of nutrients. Without earthworms, your plants would be less able to take in nitrogen and their roots would wither. Earthworms also process organic matter like compost and manure so it's more usable for microbes.

   There are three ways you can find how many earthworms your garden has:

   🌢 **Search:** It may seem basic, but you can start by just looking for earthworms on the surface of your garden. Without disrupting the soil too much, overturn some rocks and see how many creepy crawlers are moving around; while not an exact count, this can give you a rough estimate of your garden's worm population.

   🌢 **Powdered Mustard:** While humans may love a bit of mustard on their burger or hotdog, earthworms absolutely can't stand the stuff. By marking off one area of your garden and pouring in a mixture of mustard and water, earthworms will rise to the surface to escape the smell and you can count them.

   🌢 **Soil Sample:** Probably the most complicated earthworm test, getting a soil sample means digging out a six inch by six inch square of your garden to a depth of six inches and placing it in a large container. You can then sift through and individually pick out each worm. You'll want to have at least five worms for that area of garden; any less, and your plants may be suffering.

3. **The Basic Perc Test:** Water moves through your soil in a process called percolation. Basically, without soil percolation, your garden won't be able to drain properly,

and your plants will be deprived of oxygen. In addition to drowning, they will also be more susceptible to diseases. A basic 'perc test' can show you how percolated your soil is by testing a small section of your garden's drainage capabilities. By taking out a 12" by 12" section of soil and filling it with water, you can measure the rate at which the water is absorbed. You want to shoot for about 2" per hour, but anything from 1" to 3" is fine. If your soil isn't draining properly, you'll need to add more organic matter.

4. **The Ribbon Test:** The ribbon test will help you see what type of texture your soil has, ranging from heavy clay to loam, and all the way to sandy. For this you simply take a handful of soil and mix it with water. Mold the mixture until it's a uniform piece, and see what length the piece will reach before it breaks. You can then reference a texture chart to see what type of texture your garden has.

5. **The Compaction Test:** If your soil is too compacted, the roots of your plants will have a tough time growing. Testing your garden's compaction can show you how much air, water, and fertilizer is getting through. To do this test, all you'll need is a wire flag; by pushing the flag vertically down into the soil, you can see where it starts to bend. If the flag starts to bend before you reach 12", your soil is likely too compact.

Change Your Soil's pH

If your soil is too acidic, you'll want to adjust the pH to try to get it as neutral as possible. There are a couple of easy ways to adjust your pH balance, involving different materials and organic mixtures.

◗ **Bone Meal:** A great source of nutrients like calcium, bone meal can be a good way to slowly raise the pH levels of your soil. While bone meal definitely works if you give it enough time, it's best used for soils that only have a slightly lower pH balance. If your soil is incredibly acidic, it's best to use one of the more aggressive materials to fix the problem. You'll want to use about one pound of bone meal for every ten square feet of your garden, but this is just a rough estimate. If your soil is a bit more acidic, feel free to use more.

- **Lime:** While not as great as the lime we need for margaritas, limestone is a very useful way to increase your garden's pH at a slightly higher rate than with bone meal. You'll want to get a specific kind of limestone known as dolomite limestone. Some stores will list it as garden or agricultural lime; whatever name it goes by, this particular type is perfect for pH adjustments. Depending on your garden's current acidity, you'll want to use between ½ and 2 pounds of lime per square foot.

- **Wood Ash:** wood ash is a great organic material to use when trying to neutralize your garden's pH, and is especially effective in the cooler months like fall. Be careful what kind of wood you choose: you'll want to make sure that any wood ash you use came from a non-treated source. You'll also want to ensure you don't use black walnut, which can be particularly toxic to certain types of plants.

- **Compost:** While compost won't have the same pH effect as lime or wood ash, it is a great way to maintain healthy pH over a longer period of time. Compost doesn't pack quite the same punch as some of these other materials, but it does have a much wider range of auxiliary benefits. While your pH balances, compost will provide vital nutrients to encourage stronger plant growth. Again, this isn't going to deal with an acidity problem quickly; if your pH balance is way out of whack, it's probably better to go with limestone or organic wood ash.

Avoid Soil Compaction and Disruption

Soil compaction and disruption are always detrimental to healthy soil, and you'll want to make sure you do both as little as possible. Compaction is a natural by-product of moving around and tending to your garden, with certain soil types like heavy clay being more susceptible to being compacted. You'll want to make sure you have well-defined pathways to avoid compacting soil near your plants roots, otherwise they may struggle to grow. As for disruption, you may be tempted to dig below the surface of your garden. If your soil isn't healthy, you'll probably want to find clues as to why this is happening; getting deeper into the dirt seems like a logical way to do this. In actuality, your soil is an entire ecosystem all its own, and disrupting that ecosystem can interrupt the flow of oxygen, water, and nutrients to your plants. This has led to popularization of techniques like no-dig gardening, which reduce the amount of interaction a gardener has with their soil in an effort to make their garden more self-sustained.

Put in More Organic Matter

Our gardens would be nothing without organic matter, and adding in more will almost always be a great idea. One of the best organic materials for your garden is compost, a wonderful mixture of recyclable ingredients you can get from your garden or kitchen. There is a variety of materials you can put in compost, including food or vegetable scraps, yard trimmings, and certain paper products. You'll want to avoid using animal products, coal, or diseased plants in your compost, as these can actually do your garden harm.

There are a number of things compost can do to make your garden healthier, including:

- Break down existing organic matter
- Make the soil more nutrient rich
- Reduce the need for chemical fertilizers
- Help ward away animals and harmful pests
- Reduce the chance of your plants becoming diseased
- Produce helpful bacteria and fungi

Also err on the side of excess when it comes to compost. It would be pretty hard to have too much in your garden, and unless your plants are so covered they can't get water or sunlight, it doesn't hurt to add a bit more.

How to Make Your Own Compost

There are **five basic steps** to creating your own compost:

1. **Choose Your Type:** There are a few different types of compost piles you can use for your garden, including the traditional pile or a compost bin. A compost pile is simple enough to create: just leave your ingredients in an outside open air space, exposing them to the elements. This will generally work, but wind, rain, and animals can all damage your compost pile and leave your plants without the natural fertilizer they crave.

   A better option is usually to use a compost bin, which can range from constructing your own DIY garbage can bin to purchasing the most expensive one available from your local home and garden store. The latter is really not necessary: a DIY bin will function almost the same, and with the right care, your compost will be just as good as with costlier options.

2. **Choose Your Location:** Particularly important if you choose the open air compost pile, choosing the location of your compost will involve identifying what will be the most protected and the most convenient. You'll want somewhere that doesn't receive too much natural rain, as this can affect the compost negatively. The ideal spot will be dry and shady, and somewhere you can easily transfer the completed compost to your soil.

3. **Select Your Materials:** I briefly mentioned a few kinds of materials you can use in your compost, but when looking at what you'll add to your pile, think in terms of "brown" vs "green". Green materials will have higher levels of nitrogen, while brown materials will be higher in carbon. There are so many different things you can put in compost to make it rich and biodiverse. The exact ratio of brown to green in compost is a highly debated subject. Some say it should be as high as 30:1 brown to green, while others say it should only be 4:1 brown to green. Whatever the perfect ratio is, most all agree that you should have more brown than green. A few items I personally put in my compost include:

Eggshells	Coffee filters and grounds
Paper products like cardboard and newspapers	Tea bags
	Wood chips
Grass and yard trimmings	Cotton
	Wool
Food and vegetable scraps	
Plant roots and leaves	

4. **Aerate and Monitor Your Compost:** Maintaining your compost will help keep it producing high quality humus, and aeration is a major part of this upkeep. This process makes sure that your compost pile has enough oxygen to allow decomposition to take place. You'll want to turn the pile over about once a week in the summer months, and one to two times a month in the winter months. You'll also want to keep track of the temperature, as a good compost pile should be running over 120-130 degrees Fahrenheit. Compost piles can reach as high as 150 degrees Fahrenheit at their peak, which shouldn't be a cause for concern. Once your compost begins to cool off, that's how you know it's almost done.

5. **Once Complete, Integrate it into Your Soil:** You'll know your compost is ready once it becomes dark brown or black in appearance, crumbly in texture, and it has a slightly sweet smell when sifted. You also should see no evidence of the ingredients you initially put in, as these should all have broken down during the process of decomposition. Once you are sure the compost is ready, spread it in a layer between one and three inches thick on the top of your soil. This should be done once or twice a growing season, with early fall being the most optimal time to do so.

You can also mix the compost in, but this would go against certain techniques like no-dig gardening. Digging into the soil can disturb microorganisms and reduce nutrient access by root systems. That being said, with more clay-heavy or sandy soils, adding compost by mixing it directly in can be worth it. What steps you take to keep your garden as healthy as possible depend on your specific goals. If your soil has the right texture, putting the compost on top is usually the best choice. But if your particular soil type requires more amendment, it's perfectly fine to mix the compost in a bit deeper.

From the Ground to the Sky

Getting the right soil in place is like the foundation to a good house— very important, but hardly the most exciting step in building a home. You'll need to find out how to fuel your home with electricity, as well as get a system of pipes running through your house so your faucets don't run dry. Your garden is much the same way: it needs energy and water to thrive, and you sometimes have to be the one to provide it. Finding out how much sunlight and water your plants need is vital to their survival; a regular schedule for both will make sure your vegetables grow large and plentifully. In our next chapter, we'll look at the different sunlight intensities plants need, the benefits of a regular watering schedule, and what happens if you fall short.

Chapter 5

Let there be Light... and Water!

How Long Can a Vegetable Plant Live Without Water?

How important is water, really? Well, your average fully-grown vegetable plant is a big fan of water. So much so, in fact, that they can only last **between four and seven days** without it before they completely wither and die. Of course, the type of plant and how healthy your soil is can change this time a bit, but for the most part, a week is the maximum amount of time before you'll need to bury that plant for good.

If your garden is a vehicle, and organic matter is the fuel, then water and light are the regular maintenance you perform to keep your car on the road. Having a regular watering schedule and ensuring your plants get enough sunlight can mean the difference between a beautiful and productive green space or a sad patch of dirt and weeds. It may seem simple: give the plants a little water, let them sit in the sun, and boom – vegetable city. Unfortunately, it takes a bit more effort to introduce these elements in the correct way. I had my own struggles in the beginning with striking a good balance, leading to me wasting almost an entire growing season.

I'll admit when I first started out, I occasionally got a bit ahead of myself when it came to what I was capable of. Remember when I told you I planted far too big a garden to keep up with? Well, sometimes we have to make mistakes more than once to understand where we went wrong. A different growing season, a bit further into my experience, I once again embarked on a quest to create a farmers' market worth of vegetables. But aha! This time, I made sure not to plant any competing species next to each other. Unfortunately, I still wasn't able to give each plant the care it needed, and I knew very little about what my vegetables needed for sunlight and water. I knew they *needed* both, obviously. But in my naivety, I thought that simply having both was enough. Boy was I wrong!

I hadn't observed which parts of my garden received more sunlight, and put my vegetables in neat rows based more on what they were growing close to. I made sure to pay close attention as I sequestered my brassicas far apart, keeping my cabbage to one section of my garden and my cauliflower to another. But what I didn't notice was that creeping line of light moving across my soil every day after sunrise. My lettuce and spinach seemed to be withering in their sunny spots, while tomatoes and corn seemed to be struggling in the shade. All of my veggies received some level of sunlight; that much I knew to be necessary. But it turns out that lettuce and spinach are full-shade veggies, and tomatoes and corn are full-sun plants. You may be saying "Well what does this mean?" I'll go into detail about that below. For the purpose of the story, it basically means I had not given them the growing environment they needed.

I faced a similar problem with watering. My soil at the time was clay heavy, but I didn't really consider how that would affect my watering schedule. I watered the garden in the same pattern I had with my previous one, even though that was a bit of a sandier mixture. Shockingly, my soil seemed waterlogged! Turns out, watering isn't as simple as just keeping an area moisturized: certain types of soil hold water, and other types drain it quickly. This too hindered my plants' growth. With the sun and water complications combined, the growing season overall was a bit of a disaster.

It seems like the most straightforward part of gardening: plants need sun, and plants need water. But as experience shows us, almost no part of gardening is as easy as it seems. When it comes to sunlight and water, your plants are going to produce way more come harvest time if you get the conditions exactly right.

Let's start with sunlight, and the different types of intensity your plants need.

Different Levels of Sun Exposure

There are four primary types of sunlight intensity plants fall into: **full sun**, **part sun**, **part shade**, and **full shade**.

- **Full Sun:** Plants in this category should be in the sunniest part of your garden and are often resistant to high-heat and low-moisture environments. This isn't a hard and fast rule, as there are some full-sun plants that can still survive in rainier regions. For the most part, these plants need at least six hours of direct sunlight every day. This means if you intend to use companion planting with full-sun plants, make sure they don't grow near companions that could block out that precious sunlight.

- **Part Sun:** These plants require a bit less sun, either receiving more filtered sunlight or direct sun for only part of the day. For these plants, you'll want to choose a part of your garden that gets direct sunlight either in the morning or the afternoon, but not both (keeping in mind that sunlight in the afternoon is usually more intense.) Part-sun plants need between three and six hours of direct sunlight, but it's usually best to avoid the intense light present in the middle of the day.

- **Part Shade:** Similar to part-sun plants, part-shade plants should receive less sunlight and tend to dislike the intense sunlight that plants can get in the middle of the day. You'll want these plants to get a few hours in the morning or afternoon, or a longer period of time with more filtered sunlight. Just like part-sun plants, part-shade plants need between three and six hours of sunlight per day. While it is optional to avoid direct sunlight with part-sun plants, part-shade plants almost always need to be protected during the intensity of midday.

🖊 **Full Shade:** Full-shade plants will need to be guarded from direct sunlight to varying degrees, depending on what type of species you choose to plant. Certain species of ferns, for example, must be kept almost entirely in the shade for the majority of their lives. Other plants can handle light filtered through trees, or the indirect sunlight found in the morning and evening. For the most part, these plants cannot handle the direct sunlight of midday. Overall, full-shade plants should get less than three hours of sunlight per day.

What is Dappled Sunlight?

When we talk about "dappled" (or "filtered") sunlight, we're referring to the indirect light plants receive through the filter of trees or during the hours the sun isn't hanging in the middle of the sky. Plants in the full-shade, part-shade, or part-sun category will likely thrive with this type of light; you'll want to see what areas of your garden receive dappled sunlight and record which areas will work best for shadier species. The process of measuring sunlight isn't too complicated, and can be completed over the course of a day or two.

Measuring Sunlight Exposure in Your Garden

The first step to determining how much sunlight exposure your garden receives is to separate it into sections. This will depend heavily on what layout of garden you chose, but try to set boundaries based on where your house, fence, and trees are placed in your backyard. Areas closer to your fence will naturally receive more shade when the sun is on the other side, as well the parts of the garden near your home. Sections with trees, on the other hand, will probably get more dappled sunlight as it filters through the leaves.

Once you've established clear boundary markers, create a chart separating each section with a box showing each hour from sunrise to sunset. Observe your garden over the course of the day, writing down whether the area is receiving full sunlight, dappled sunlight, or full shade. If you like, do this for a couple of days to see how certain cloud cover or conditions affect the sunlight. Once you're done, you'll be able to see precisely where certain plants will thrive, and further plan out which companion plants you'll want in each area.

Another fun way to measure sunlight exposure is with a timelapse camera. I'm not suggesting that you run out and buy a $500 GoPro just to see how sunny your garden is, but if you happen to have one already, you can point it at your garden and see the movement of the sun throughout the day. If you place a clock in the frame, it makes it very easy to see exactly when each part of your garden is getting sunlight and what kind.

Vegetables and Their Sunlight Requirements

There is an almost endless variety of vegetables you can plant in different sunlight conditions. Let's break down some of your choices for each sunlight type.

Full-Shade Vegetables

- Arugula
- Endive
- Kale
- Brussels sprouts
- Bok choy
- Lettuce
- Swiss chard
- Mustard greens
- Spinach

Part-Sun/Part-Shade Vegetables

- Artichoke
- Asparagus
- Beans
- Mint
- Onions
- Oregano
- Parsley
- Cauliflower
- Celery
- Chives
- Cilantro
- Beets
- Coriander
- Garlic
- Leek
- Pea
- Radish
- Rutabaga
- Shallots
- Turnips
- Broccoli
- Cabbage
- Carrots
- Cardoon

Full-Sun Vegetables

- Tomatoes
- Watermelon
- Cantaloupe
- Corn
- Okra
- Basil
- Cucumbers
- Eggplant
- Peppers
- Squash
- Sweet potatoes
- Yams
- Taro
- Cassava
- Peas
- Yard-long beans
- Sunflowers
- Malabar spinach
- Water spinach (kangkong)

The Water Factor

Just as important as proper sunlight exposure, keeping your plants hydrated is essential to their growth. Without water, your seeds won't sprout, nutrients won't be able to travel throughout your plants, and they won't be able to complete the process of photosynthesis. Giving your garden the correct amount of water starts by understanding what type of soil you have, and what the particular hydration needs of that soil are.

Understanding Your Soil Type

We touched on soil types in a previous chapter, but to reiterate, soil is made up of a mixture of sand, silt, and clay. The combination of these three components your garden contains will determine how much water it needs to stay moisturized. Clay soil, for example, drains much more slowly than other soil types. Because it holds onto water for a longer period of time, you'll want to water a garden with clay soil less frequently. Sandy soil, on the other hand, will drain much more quickly; with this soil type, if you don't stay on top of watering, you may find your soil drying out.

How Much Water Do My Vegetables Need?

Part of knowing how much water your vegetables need is, again, knowing the type of soil. If you have a clay-heavy garden, you'll want to water your plants about once a week. This of course depends on what type of weather your area is having, and how much rainfall has already occurred. If your soil is sandier, you may want to water your garden twice a week. Vegetables need moisture, and a sandy garden could deprive their roots of the hydration they need.

Keep Track of Rainwater

How much rainfall your area receives is a huge factor in keeping your garden at the right level of moisture. The logic here isn't too complicated: if your climate involves frequent rainfall, you'll water less; if there is rarely rain, then you'll need to supplement with more water on your own. Of course, in practice, it isn't that simple. You'll want to keep track of how much rainwater your garden receives so you can more precisely attune to your plants' needs. The easiest way to do this is with a rain gauge, which will measure rain in inches so you can adjust your watering schedule accordingly.

Be as Efficient as Possible

Watering your plants is important, but just as important is avoiding waste. Overwatering your plants will not only wash out nutrients and stunt their growth, but it could lead to a shockingly high water bill at the end of the month. You'll want to use an efficient method of watering, like drip irrigation, to save time and money. Drip irrigation involves using either a series of perforated hoses or an automated system to gradually water your plants over time. This way you don't saturate only the top layer of the soil and instead spread the moisture out evenly for every plant in your garden.

Pack in the Mulch Power

Part of the watering process actually doesn't involve water at all. If you want to slow down the drainage of your soil, you can do so by adding biodegradable mulch.

Biodegradable Mulch: Organic material (such as decaying leaves, bark, or compost) spread around or over a plant to enrich or insulate the soil.

Whether you use dried leaves, grass clippings, wood chips, or any other organic material, mulch will hold on to moisture and release it slowly over time. This lets the roots drink up their fill without being overwhelmed. Mulch can also help regulate temperatures by acting as a layer of insulation. This prevents the heat from evaporating all the water within your soil, further aiding in hydration.

Putting mulch on your garden is easy: just spread a layer about two to five inches thick on the top of your soil, depending on how much moisture your garden needs to retain. Try to avoid letting the mulch directly contact your plant stems to avoid rot, and be careful not to overdo it: if the mulch gets too thick, it may actually prevent water from getting to the roots due to its moisture-retention abilities.

Ways to Water Your Garden

There are a few ways to water your garden, and the method you choose really depends on personal preference and the size of your green space. Proper watering is about getting the water down deep into the soil, so those thirsty roots can drink their fill. This doesn't mean disturbing the soil and running hoses below ground; the process of percolation will take care of that for you. By saturating the top layer of the soil, moisture will trickle down for several inches and reach your garden's roots.

As far as the implement you use, you'll want to choose based on how big your garden is. If you have a smaller space, you don't need much more than a watering can or hose with a nozzle attachment. Avoid anything with a harsh spray, as this can move the soil around and accidentally expose root systems. If you have a denser gardening space (which is likely if you are considering companion planting), you can use trench systems to make sure the water flow goes where you want it. This involves digging little moats around each plant and laying hoses directly on the ground so the water cascades down each trench. You can use boards or rocks to help reduce the erosion from this method as well.

We touched on drip irrigation before, but if you have a larger garden, this will be the method you want to use. I have recently upgraded my gardening space, and drip irrigation is the way I make sure my plants get just the right amount of moisture. You can make your own DIY drip irrigation system with little more than a hose and drill with a 1/16" bit: start by measuring the distance between your plants, then make markings on your hose so the holes are the proper distance apart. Drill the holes, hook up the hose, and voila! You have your own drip irrigation system.

Water Table: How to Ensure Your Vegetables Stay Hydrated

While there isn't space to list every single vegetable you may grow in your garden, I've assembled a couple of the stand-bys I find myself planting season after season. This chart will look at the type of vegetable being planted, how much water is needed, and what the most critical time for watering would be.

Vegetable Type	How Much Water is Needed in Gallons (Per 5 Foot Row)	Most Critical Watering Time
Broccoli	Between three and five per week	During the first four weeks after transplanting
Carrots	Three per week when first planted, rising to six per week as the roots mature	Whenever the soil begins to get too dry (carrots will die quickly in very dry soil)

Cabbage	Six per week	Whenever the weather gets especially hot and dry
Beans	Six per week	During pod and flower formation, as well as picking
Beets	Three per week	Any time the soil is getting very dry
Brussel Sprouts	Between three to five per week	Consistently for the first four weeks after transplanting
Cauliflower	Six per week	Consistently throughout the cauliflower's lifespan
Celery	Six per week	Consistently throughout the growing season
Cucumbers	A minimum of three per week	Consistently throughout the growing season
Corn	Six per week	Whenever tassels are forming and when the cobs begin to swell
Leafy Greens (Like Lettuce or Spinach)	Two per week	Consistently throughout the growing season

Parsnips	No more than three per week	Whenever the soil is getting too dry
Onions	Three per week	During the beginning stages of planting
Peppers	Between three and six per week	Consistently throughout the growing season
Potatoes	Between three and six per week	When the potatoes are about the size of a cocktail onion (about 40 days after planting)
Peas	Three per week	During flower and pod formation, as well as picking
Tomatoes	Six per week	For the first three to four weeks after transplanting, and again when the tomatoes begin to form
Squashes	Three per week	Consistently throughout the growing season
Radishes	Between three and six per week	Consistently throughout the growing season

You Want Light and Water... But What You Don't Want is Pests

Now that we've touched on the elements your garden needs to succeed, let's talk about what it doesn't need: pests. Harmful bugs can be the bane of good garden growth, and the wrong insects can even ward away the beneficial ones you need to help your plants thrive. In Chapter 6, we'll go into companion planting solutions to this pest problem, and how you can use certain species to repel unwanted garden guests and attract good ones.

Chapter 6

The Good, the Bad, and the Ugly: Using Companion Planting to Naturally Drive Away Harmful Bugs and Attract Beneficial Ones

Ten Fun Facts About Garden Insects

1. It takes honeybees almost ten million trips to get enough nectar to make a single pound of honey.

2. While grasshoppers see your crops as food, many parts of the world see *them* as food. Grasshoppers are a major part of the diet of many people living in Africa and Asia.

3. Ladybugs are one of the best beneficial garden insects to have, mostly due to the war they wage on aphids. A single ladybug can eat up to 50 aphids in a day, with most ladybugs eating thousands of aphids over their lifetime.

4. Praying mantises are great insects to have if you want to clear away bad bugs, but did you know they also know the future? Well, not exactly, but their name "Mantis" does come from the Greek word for "prophet."

5. While no human likes the smell of a stink bug, other stink bugs love it. Their distinctive scent is actually part of a biological process designed to attract potential mates.

6. Green lacewings can help take down a pest population, but why do they have their distinctive green coloring? It's actually part of their camouflage, helping them blend into your garden and hide from predators.

7. Aphids, one of the more annoying pests, have developed an alarm pheromone that signals other aphids when they are being attacked. Luckily, certain species of beetle have learned this smell, and follow it to find an easy aphid prey.

8. Pill bugs, doodle bugs, rollie pollies – whatever you call them, these little guys are a frequent resident in many

gardens. You may think they'd be related to other common garden insects like crickets, but actually, pill bugs are more closely related to shrimp and lobster.

9. Wasps can be a scary adversary to meet head on, and it's easy to think they don't offer many benefits to your garden. The truth is, some wasps can actually help carry pollen to plants to help them grow.

10. Butterflies have built in compasses, allowing them to detect which direction is north. This helps them fly south during their fall migration.

Much like sunlight and water, creepy crawlers are an essential part of a good growing environment. Beneficial insects help pollinate plants, take down pests, and attract other bugs that can improve your garden's ecosystem. These benefits, particularly pest control, can help you avoid using artificial or chemical solutions to common gardening problems. One big issue that organic gardeners face is the question of pesticides; pesticides can be harmful to your plants and the surrounding wildlife, and can be dangerous to humans.

Five Reasons to Avoid Chemical Pesticides at All Costs

Reason #1: Pesticides Can Be Harmful to Humans

According to the Environmental Protection Agency or EPA, chemical pesticides can have a direct effect on the human nervous system. Their studies have also shown that some pesticides contain carcinogens, and can damage hormone and endocrine systems. Pesticides are also poisonous, with exposure irritating the skin and eyes. Consumption can result in gastrointestinal issues and even death in some cases.

Reason #2: Pets Are at Risk Too

As a dog owner, I would never let my pet anywhere near a garden with chemical pesticides. Dogs are naturally curious animals, and there will be no stopping them from galloping through your garden from time to time. Licking, sniffing, and even residual contact with the animal's fur can all introduce pesticides into their system. This also applies if your pets eat a wild animal that's ingested pesticides; if your cat likes to hunt mice, for example, an infected mouse could easily poison your feline.

Reason #3: Chronic Pesticide Exposure Can Have Long-Term Effects

Even if you don't make direct contact with pesticides, long-term exposure can slowly damage your internal organs and bodily systems. Some studies have shown that even your blood cells can be affected, with common damage centers being the liver, kidneys, and peripheral nervous system.

Reason #4: Pesticides Hurt Helpful Insects

While companion planting offers a gentler way of dissuading insects, chemical pesticides don't distinguish between friend and foe. Pollinators are most affected by chemical pesticides, with bees, flies and butterflies often being the first beneficial insects to fall. Without pollinators, your plants can't grow, so it's in your best interest to keep them safe.

Reason #5: Chemical Pesticides Can Kill Wildlife

While you may want to dissuade certain animal species from getting into your garden, you by no means want them dead. Gardening is an appreciation of the natural world, and wildlife has just as much right to exist in your backyard as you do. Unfortunately, harmful pesticides can be consumed by wildlife accidentally, injuring or killing them in the process. This can lower the birth rates for their species, even causing their ecosystems to collapse if problems persist long enough. Chemical pesticides can also leak into water sources, creating another way that animals can accidentally consume them.

The "Good Guys": Beneficial Bugs to Get Your Garden Going

There are three primary kinds of beneficial insects:

- **Pollinators:** Like their name implies, these bugs are responsible for spreading pollen to our plants, allowing them to flower and grow. Pollinators include familiar insects like butterflies, bees, moths, and flies.

- **Predators:** While pollinators encourage garden growth through the gentler method of pollination, predators are a bit more aggressive. These insects deter, attack, or eat malicious garden pests, and include bugs like praying mantids, green lacewings, and ladybugs.

- **Parasites:** Parasites assist your garden in a similar way to predators, but with somewhat more insidious methods. Parasites lay eggs near or inside bad insects; when these eggs hatch, the larvae will use the bad insects *as food.* Scary, I know, but hey, better them than your plants!

There are many bugs that fall into each of these categories, including:

- **Ladybugs and Ladybug Larvae:** From the time they are born to the time they die, ladybugs are aphid-killing machines. Even as larvae, ladybugs have been known to eat up to 40 aphids in a single hour. As adults, these spotted insects will eat mites, mealybugs, leafhoppers, and even the eggs of harmful insects. If you want to keep your garden protected, ladybugs are a must.

- **Green Lacewings and Lacewing Larvae:** Much like ladybugs, lacewings are insects that dedicate their lives to eradicating garden pests. Whether in the larval stage or fully grown, the green lacewing will eat aphids, mites, leafhoppers, mealybugs, whiteflies, and caterpillars. They've even been known to help spread pollen from flowers, though their main focus is dispatching garden foes.

- **Parasitic Wasps:** Parasitic wasps have the unique ability to introduce parasites to a variety of insect eggs, including tomato hornworms, codling moths, cabbage loopers, cabbage worms, and corn borers. They also eat scale, whiteflies, sawfly larvae, leaf miners, caterpillars, and aphids.

- **Hoverflies and Robber Flies:** Hoverflies and robber flies share similar prey, with both being excellent at controlling beetles, caterpillars, aphids, and thrips. Robber flies are also adept at killing grasshoppers, leafhoppers, and harmful wasps. In addition to their pest control benefits, hoverflies are excellent at pollination, and feed on pollen and nectar.

- **Ground Beetles:** Ground beetles help add 24-hour security to your garden, looking for prey even in the late hours of the evening or middle of the night. Beetles have a wide range of prey; both adult beetles and larvae are adept at consuming snails, slugs, mites, caterpillars, cutworms, earwigs, vine borers, and aphids.

- **Mantids:** Mantids, primarily the praying mantis, are a mixed bag. Yes, they can help take down some bigger pests, and some have been known to take down far larger insects and animals (most notably cockroaches and small rodents.) Unfortunately, this predatory instinct isn't restricted to harmful insects, and a praying mantis is just as likely to kill a butterfly or bee as it is a mosquito.

◐ **Common Garden Spiders:** Spiders are all around pest-catching machines, quickly eliminating flies, wasps, beetles, mosquitos, and aphids. Their webs can help catch a large number of pests quickly, as opposed to some other beneficial insects who need to catch them one by one. Spiders do however have a downside. They also catch beneficial insects.

◐ **Butterflies:** Butterflies are excellent at pollination: by feeding off of flower nectar and floating from plant to plant, butterflies lightly dust your garden's inhabitants with the pollen they need. A good number of butterflies in your growing space is also an indicator of overall garden health.

◐ **Assassin Bugs:** Assassin bugs primarily help in dispatching insects that harm your plant's foliage. Their main targets are caterpillars and grasshoppers, which will gnaw on your plant's leaves, damaging their ability to photosynthesize and transport nutrients. This in turn leads to stunted growth, and less production when harvest season comes. Assassin bugs will help tackle this problem.

◐ **Bees:** Bees are responsible for pollinating 80% of all flowering plants on the planet earth, with a single bee pollinating up to 300 million flowers every day. It's not hard to see why you'd want these insects in your garden; pollination is a necessary component for many plants to flower and flourish, so you'll want to keep your bee friends close.

What Should I Plant to Attract These Beneficial Bugs?

There are a variety of plant species you'll want to put in your garden to attract beneficial insects, including low-growing plants like rosemary, mint, and thyme. These will give insects like ground beetles the camouflage they need to move about your garden undisturbed, consuming pests without worrying about predators. Insects also like areas where they can safely lay their eggs, so establishing a small corner with shadier plants could give them the protection they need.

Plants that have small flowers, like angelica, coriander, dill, fennel, Queen Anne's lace, clovers, rue, and yarrow will also encourage smaller wasps to inhabit your garden. These wasps can help carry small amounts of pollen while dealing with bigger caterpillars and other bugs, generally feeding on their larvae. Composite flowers will attract wasps as well, like daisy and chamomile, while mint and catnip will help bring in hoverflies and robber flies.

If you want to see a more comprehensive list of companion plants to help bring in beneficial bugs, refer to the section in Chapter 1 titled "6 Bugs You Want On Your Team."

Specific Plant Types to Put in Your Companion Garden

- **Eggplant** (*Solanum melongena*): A delicious vegetable, rich in antioxidants and fiber, eggplant will help bring in insects (like predatory mites) that will help eat red spider mites, which can cause damage to plant tissue and foliage.

- **Fern-Leaf Yarrow** (*Achillea filipendulina*): A full-sun plant that thrives in sandy soil, the fern-leaf yarrow grows well in hot areas with less access to water. Not only that, but fern-leaf yarrow will attract the queen of aphid killers: the ladybug.

- **Coriander** (*Coriandrum sativum*): Coriander is an essential spice for any Latin-American dish, and nothing beats adding fresh coriander to your enchiladas. This spice is great at attracting trichogramma wasps, which can kill hundreds of different types of garden pest including the wax moth, tomato hornworm, cabbage looper, codling moth, various types of borer (European corn, peach, and squash), armyworm, bagworm, cutworm, earworm, and alfalfa caterpillar.

- **Lavender Globe Lily** (*Allium tanguticum*): A beautiful mixture of purple flowers and dark green leaves, the lavender globe lily will brighten up your garden and attract hoverflies. Next to ladybugs and lacewings, hoverflies are one of the main killers of aphids. They are also effective against caterpillars, scales, and thrips.

- **'Lemon Gem' Marigold** (*Tagetes tenuifolia*): Also known as the signet marigold or golden marigold, this type of flower is common in Central America, Mexico, Colombia, and Peru. They are a very low-maintenance plant, and can help repel harmful insects like burrowing insects and mosquitos. Their distinct scent can even ward away small animals!

- **Tansy** (*Tanacetum vulgare*): Tansys can add a gorgeous yellow hue to your green space, though they have no distinguishable smell. This attribute actually works in the tansy's favor, helping it attract tachinid flies. These parasites feast on various kinds of caterpillars, cabbage worms, cabbage loopers, army worms, cutworms, and corn earworms, as well as stink bugs, beetles, fly larvae, and squash bug nymphs.

- **Peter Pan Goldenrod** (*Solidago virgaurea*): Common in Asia, North America, Europe, and South America, the Peter Pan goldenrod is often used in tea for its medicinal benefits. It also helps attract beetles, bees, flies, moths and butterflies, which all enjoy snacking on the goldenrod plant for sustenance.

◗ **Spearmint** (*Mentha spicata*): A great mint to grow in almost any climate, spearmint is a part-shade plant that produces a highly aromatic oil. This spearmint oil acts as a natural pesticide, especially potent against moths. It also attracts damsel bugs, which mainly consume aphids and caterpillars.

◗ **Crimson Thyme** (*Thymus serpyllum coccineus*): Crimson thyme is a full-sun plant that enjoys sandier soil, thriving in drier climates that get less natural rainfall. This species of thyme also attracts mini-wasps, which are effective killers of a number of annoying garden pests, although they also kill honey bees.

◗ **White Sweet Alyssum** (*Lobularia maritima*): Coming in various colors including pink, violet, rose-red, white, and lilac, white sweet alyssum is so named for the sweet scent its petals give off. This scent attracts braconid wasps, which are particularly skilled at taking out the hornworm.

◗ **Dill** (*Anethum graveolens*): The best foundation for any good tzatziki sauce or potato salad, dill is an herb native to Asia and the Mediterranean. It is very good at attracting a diverse array of beneficial insects, including mealybug destroyers, aphid midges, ladybugs, green lacewings, braconid wasps, tachinid flies, and hoverflies.

Bad Bugs, Bad Bugs, What You Gonna Do?

We've looked at which insects you want in your garden and how to get them there, but what about damaging insects? There are many pests that want nothing more than to see you fail in your gardening pursuits; these obnoxious critters will consume your budding plants, scare away beneficial bugs, and bring in harmful diseases.

- **Caterpillars:** A hungry caterpillar can be the bane of your garden's existence: their appetite is ferocious, and a single caterpillar can punch holes in your foliage, destroy stems and stalks, and consume your plant's precious leaves.

- **Aphids:** The sworn enemy of vegetables, fruits, trees, and flowers, aphids will suck the life out of your garden if left unchecked. By draining plants of their sap, aphids cause the decay and collapse of vegetables' structural integrity. Aphids will also increase the growth rate of mildew, and can introduce all kinds of viral diseases into your garden.

- **Slugs and Snails:** Slow, methodical and slimy slugs and snails may not move quickly but can do damage to your garden in no time. These insects prefer damp or shaded conditions, and will often hide amongst your low-lying plants. Not only will they damage your greenery, but they can be harmful to your pets as well!

- **Codling Moth:** Codling moths will often be found around fruit, particularly apples. Adult codling moths will burrow into apples to lay their larvae. You know that common trope in cartoons, when a character bites into an apple and finds a squirming critter within? That was most likely a codling moth larva!

- **Flea Beetles:** With the mobility of fleas and the hard carapace of beetles, flea beetles are a terrifying garden guest to discover. This type of malicious beetle is particularly harmful to young plants; by feeding directly on their roots, they can impede or completely stop a new plant's progress.

- **Vine Weevil:** Enemy to indoor and outdoor plants alike, the vine weevil is a common garden pest that loves to snack on leaves. Like the flea beetle, vine weevils will also attack plants at their roots, cutting off their nutrient supply and causing them to wither.

🍃 **Leaf Miners:** Getting their namesake from their preferred food, leaves, leaf miners will leave trails of discoloration along the surface of your plants' leaves. This isn't the biggest problem in the world; the damage done on the leaf only affects its aesthetics, and doesn't actually harm the plants' ability to grow. But if you want a good-looking garden, it may be best to get these little guys out of there.

What Should I Plant to Repel These Bad Bugs?

🍃 **Basil** (*Ocimum basilicum*): Basil is a big ingredient in Italian cooking, and a great herb to add to your repertoire. In addition to being delicious, basil also helps drive away aphids, spider mites, and white flies. Basil is especially effective when planted around tomatoes, helping deter hornworm moths from burrowing into them.

🍃 **Onion** (*Allium cepa*): Onions are another ingredient no Italian dish can go without; their distinctive smell and taste are so good, they'll make you cry! Much like humans, bugs have trouble dealing with the fragrant aroma of onions. Whereas we will power through and chop up the vegetables for dinner, insects simply can't stand them. Onions are very good at deterring cucumber beetles, aphids, and maggot flies.

🍃 **Garlic** (*Allium sativum*): Much like onions, garlic is well known for its unique aroma and tasty flavor. With its strong scent, garlic serves as a great deterrent to spider mites, aphids, and Japanese beetles.

◗ **Lavender** (*Lavandula*): the soft scent of lavender can brighten up any home or garden, but for some reason, bugs can't stand the stuff. Lavender is great for defending vegetables like lettuce, or any type of leafy green, due to its ability to drive away aphids and whiteflies.

◗ **Parsley** (*Petroselinum crispum*): Parsley is the perfect garnish for almost any dish, adding a nice spattering of green on top of pasta, omelets, and or your favorite soup. Planting parsley early in the season can help you protect your asparagus plants due to its ability to deter asparagus beetles.

◗ **Castor-Oil Plant** (*Ricinus communis*): A slightly more dangerous option for pest relief, the castor-oil plant is very effective at keeping away much larger animals than insects. Creatures like moles and voles will dig up your roots and eat your plants whole, but not if you have castor-oil plants guarding the perimeter. A word of warning though: **these plants are poisonous to humans.** Their beans especially can cause severe gastrointestinal stress, and in high enough quantities, even death.

◗ **Tomatoes** (*Solanum lycopersicum*): While basil can help protect your tomato plants, tomatoes themselves are a great companion plant to have with cabbage and broccoli. These members of the brassica family are especially prone to housing diamondback moths, whose larvae will eat chunks out of your plants before they get a chance to produce. Fortunately, they absolutely hate tomatoes, and will usually leave any brassicas near tomatoes alone.

◗ **Catnip** (*Nepeta cataria*): Cats deserve to have fun too, and it wouldn't hurt to grow your feline friend a little patch of their favorite intoxicant: catnip! A member of the mint family, catnip isn't only good for getting your cat a bit tipsy:

the distinct smell repels adult flea beetles, which can ravage your radishes and eggplants.

- **Calamint** (*Calamintha*): Belonging to the same family as catnip, calamint is one of the main protectors of cabbage. Planting these plants in between your crops can help turn away cabbage worms and cabbage loopers, two of the main insect antagonists that can ruin a good cabbage patch.

- **Chives** (*Allium schoenoprasum*): A great addition to baked potatoes or seafood dishes, chives have a lemony scent and can add a citrus taste to a variety of meals. This same lemony scent is also what helps them repel pests, with obnoxious bugs like aphids, Japanese beetles, and mites turning at running at the smell. While humans may not think of chives as a strong-smelling plant, the aroma is so powerful it can even turn away rabbits!

You've Weeded Out the Bad Bugs, But What About… the Weeds?

Now that you have a couple of tools in your gardening arsenal to take down insect pests, it's time to talk about another antagonist that plagues every green space in the world: weeds. Bad species of weeds are a blight on your garden, soaking up sun, water, and nutrients meant for your vegetables. This can create a terrible environment for plants to attempt to grow in, and make it feel as though you aren't making any progress. At the same time, there are actually good weed species that can help your garden, acting as a sort of lower-level companion plant. Let's take a look at the good and the bad in our next chapter all about this divisive collection of plants.

Chapter 7

Weeding Between the Lines: Understanding the Role of Weeds in your Garden

When you think of weeds, the first thought that probably comes to your head is "Ugh." While I agree with the sentiment, there are actually some types of weeds you *want* in your garden. What is considered a weed in the United States could be a delicacy in other parts of the world, with many species being used as ingredients in meals or components of medical treatments. I used to think the same thing about weeds: every seed I didn't plant myself was bad, and I wanted them out of my backyard. In the process, I ended up killing many friendly species, thinking I was helping my garden out. This was a lesson I didn't learn until I had already been through several growing seasons, and it was all the more embarrassing when I realized how much useful plant material I had wasted.

I think my vendetta against weeds started early, beginning with my grandmother letting me "help" her in the backyard. While she did her best to make me feel like I was contributing, I usually just played around and got in the way. I've talked about this in my previous book a bit, but basically, my grandmother would let me pretend to spread seeds and incorrectly water the ground near her garden, telling me I was being a big help. I realized once I got older, of course, that I really wasn't helping much at all. But with weeding, I could tell the difference. Weeding was one of the tasks my grandmother gave me that I felt really contributed to her gardens. My grandmother really lit up when I showed her a big pile of pulled weeds, and I genuinely felt like I'd helped out. I think that helps explain why I can get a bit obsessive about weeding.

Unfortunately, this fixation didn't extend to my research; for years I unknowingly pulled out dandelions, chickweed, ground ivy, and many other weeds that can be eaten or used for medicinal purposes. All this time I was trying to companion plant, and I was uprooting plants that just wanted to be companions! The point of the story is to do your research beforehand; that way, you can tell the good weeds from the bad and get the maximum benefit out of your garden. But I don't need to tell you to research; you're doing it now! Let's start with five things every gardener should know about weeds.

Five Things You Need to Know About Weeds

1. What We Call "Weeds" Are Just Plants Growing in the Wrong Place

There is no official classification of what constitutes a weed, but if a species you don't want growing in your garden begins to grow anyway, it can be considered a weed. One example of this is what farmers refer to as "volunteer corn". If a farmer grows corn in a field one year, then the next year they rotate that field to soybeans, there are often corn kernels that were left behind from the previous year that will sprout and take root. Corn growing in a soybean field is a weed, even though last year it was an intended crop. What generally makes weeds a nuisance is when they compete with your other plants for nutrients, sunlight, and water. This can create a deficit for your vegetables, reducing their growth potential and making your harvest disappointing.

2. Weeds Fall into Two Main Categories: Annuals and Perennials

Like any other plants, weeds can be annual or perennial. Annual plants will only grow for one season; they will germinate, flower, seed, and then as the colder seasons of fall and winter approach, they will die. Perennials, on the other hand, will regrow every spring, but tend to have a shorter blooming period. These are the weeds that can really be a hassle, as the end of a season isn't a guarantee their infestation will end. There are two types of annual weeds:

- **Winter Annuals:** Seeding in the late parts of summer and early fall, winter annual weeds cannot stand the heat

91

of the hotter months. They will live through the winter and germinate in spring. These weeds include common chickweed, yellow rocket, annual bluegrass, and shepherd's purse.

🌱 **Summer Annuals:** Summer annual weeds complete their life cycle throughout the summer months, dying by the first frost of the fall. These weeds can be a bit more difficult to deal with, and include species like knotweed, crabgrass, and prostrate spurge.

Unlike annuals, perennials will live for multiple years, surviving even through the harsh winter months to flower again in the spring. One similarity they do share with annuals is their division into two distinct types:

🌱 **Spreading Perennials:** Beginning their lives as seeds, spreading perennials use the process of vegetative reproduction to propagate themselves throughout your garden. Vegetative reproduction works through rhizomes and stolons: rhizomes grow underneath the top layer of soil, while stolons grow above it. Any time these stem types find purchase within your garden, they begin to grow new plants. Because of the multiplicative nature of spreading perennials, a single plant can quickly give rise to dozens more. If not attended to quickly, this type of weed can overtake your garden and create a lot more work for you to deal with. Some common spreading perennials you may see include ground ivy, Canadian thistle, hedge bindweed, yellow nutsedge, and quack grass.

🌱 **Simple Perennials:** Also known as solitary perennials, simple perennials do not spread in the same manner as spreading perennials. They grow as a single entity, though you will often see them growing in close proximity to one another. Unlike spreading perennials, these root systems work independently of one another, and do not join together beneath the soil. Simple perennials are spread by seeds, and a single plant can grow for multiple years. These weeds will continue to get larger, utilizing the nutrient advantages of their tap roots (large vertical growing roots) to grow to overwhelming sizes. Common simple perennials include plantains, dandelions, and curly dock.

3. Weeds Can Serve as an Indicator of Overall Soil Health

One positive use of weeds is that they can serve as a general barometer for how your garden is doing. Weeds are like a fever: they are usually a symptom of some larger trend developing within your greenery, instead of being the entirety of the problem. Here are some common weeds, and what they may be trying to tell you.

- **Chickweed:** Chickweed is usually a sign that your soil is rich in nitrogen, has alkaline qualities, and may be a bit compacted.

- **Bindweed:** Bindweed is a plant mostly found in the arid regions of the United States, specifically the southern areas of Arizona, Texas, and New Mexico. Finding bindweed in your garden likely means your soil is dry and compacted.

- **Dandelions:** The most common weed found in the USA, the dandelion actually has a number of nutrient benefits: they can give you vital antioxidants, and help aid in digestion. But they can also indicate that your soil is overly compacted and low in calcium.

- **Crabgrass:** Crabgrass tends to grow in soil that has imbalanced or diminished nutrients; in particular, they can be a sign that your garden is low in calcium.

- **Fragile Fern:** Fragile fern is an aggressive weed, usually seeding an area heavily and creating a number of deficits for your other plants. With their billowy fronds and quick propagation, fragile ferns will remove sunlight, nutrients, and water from your soil. In addition, they usually indicate your garden may be dehydrated, as they typically only grow in dry conditions.

- **Dock:** This weed, often found in swampier regions, usually indicates that your soil is overly damp and may be draining poorly.

- **Knapweed:** With its bright purple flowers and long stems, knapweed is one of the more aesthetically pleasing weeds that can grow in your garden. It's also a positive indicator for your soil's health, as it means that your garden is rich with nutrients, primarily potassium.

- **Henbit:** Another positive health indicator for your garden, the presence of henbit means that you have high levels of nitrogen. Of course, an overabundance of henbit may mean your nutrient ratio is off and could require adjustment.

- **Knotweed:** Growing low to the ground with small green leaves, knotweed means that the soil in your garden is probably a bit too compacted.

- **Moss:** Moss tends to grow in rainier climates, and means that your garden could be overly hydrated. Moss can also be an indicator that your garden is a bit too acidic or low in nutrients.

- **Lambsquarters:** Lambsquarters has a unique appearance, with clustered green orbs lining its long stems. This interesting looking weed means that your garden is high in nitrogen.

◊ **Mustard:** If you see mustard plants growing in your garden, that could mean that your soil is high in phosphorus. It also indicates that you have sandier soil, which means your garden could be draining quickly.

◊ **Mullein:** Mullein isn't a great weed to see in your garden, as it means that your soil could have low fertility. Gardens with mullein in them also tend to be more acidic.

◊ **Wood Sorrel:** Often mistaken for clover, wood sorrel (oxalis) means that your soil is high in magnesium and low in calcium.

◊ **Ostrich Fern:** With curling fronds growing on long vertical stocks, ostrich fern is a good sign that your garden is rich in nutrients.

◊ **Pearly Everlasting:** These weeds, easily spotted due to the small white tufts of their flowers, mean that your soil is low in nutrients and, in all likelihood, too acidic.

◊ **Ox-Eye Daisies:** Ox-eye daisies (*Leucanthemum vulgare*) do well in acidic, soggy soil. Their presence could therefore mean your garden is having trouble draining water.

◊ **Plantain:** Plantain evolved to survive the impact and pressure of trampling, and can even thrive in the pathways you walk through to tend to your garden. If you find plantain in other parts of your garden, it usually means your soil is heavy in clay and quite compacted.

◊ **Purslane:** Usually growing in rich soil, purslane is edible and actually has quite a few health benefits. It also means that your garden is probably high in phosphorus.

◊ **Quackgrass:** One of the sillier names for a weed, quackgrass will usually grow in soil that is heavy in clay and compacted.

4. You Can't Keep Weeds from Growing, But There Are Ways to Control Them

Due to the way that many weeds will blow into your garden as seeds, it's difficult to stop them from growing in your soil entirely. There are a couple of ways you can reduce the amount of seeds that find their way in, starting with cleaning plants before you transplant them into your garden. Plant roots can sometimes carry tiny weed seeds that are easy to miss, until you suddenly find yourself with an infestation of unwanted plants.

Certain types of weeds with a spreading habit can be blocked with physical structures like trenches. If you dig a trench around 1.5 feet deep and place a barrier within it, any creeping roots trying to snake their way into your green space will be stopped (most of the time.)

5. The Best Way to Keep an Area Weed Free is With Cover Plants and Mulch

The key to creating a difficult growing environment for weeds is to think of them like any other plant in your garden. What do your plants need? Well, they need sunlight, water, and nutrients. If they were cut off from those elements, they would wither and die. See where I'm going with this?

You want to be a good gardener and treat your plants right, but in this case, *I need you to be a bad gardener.* Make it harder for weeds to get the components of good growth by planting companion cover plants and giving your garden a coating of mulch. Cover plants have a number of benefits, including encouraging pollinators, controlling erosion, and retaining moisture. They will also block the sunlight in any area you plant them, preventing any weed seeds from getting the light they need to start growing. There are a wide variety of cover plants to choose from, including:

- Creeping juniper
- Creeping thyme
- Ajuga
- Deadnettle
- Sedum
- Aronia
- Epimedium
- Lavender
- Mondo grass

- Dianthus
- Ferns
- Lamb's ears
- Sweet woodruff
- Irish moss
- Chamomile
- Siberian cypress
- Sweet alyssum
- Oregano

Mulching is another great way to block out the sunlight from potential weeds, as well as to catch those that float through the wind. By acting as the first layer weed seeds interact with, they never get the chance to establish roots within the soil beneath. While you can get nonorganic mulches like rubber mulch, or a tool that acts similar to mulch like a weed barrier, I prefer organic mulches. I use chipped bark, because it takes longer to break down than other mulches. It is also less likely to attract mold, to compact, or to harbor insects (or hidden weed seeds!) The one drawback is that it doesn't provide as many nutrients, but you can overcome this by with first mulching with compost or using fertilizer.

So, What Are the Benefits of Weeds?

Benefit #1: Weeds Can Attract Pollinators

Like the plants you want in your garden, weeds can be adept at attracting pollinators. This is particularly true if you don't use chemical herbicides, which have been known to be harmful to beneficial insects. There are many great pollinator-attracting plants that we consider weeds, including:

- Dandelion
- Henbit
- Chickweed
- Purple deadnettle
- Speedwell

- Goldenrod
- Daisy
- Milkweed
- Snapdragon
- Marigold

Benefit #2: Weeds Can Serve as Distractions from Your Main Plants

It may seem a bit cruel, but you can sacrifice unwanted plants to harmful insects to add a layer of protection for your garden. By choosing a sweet-smelling or tasty plant, you can divert the attention of bad bugs, who will choose the easier meal. Having an area on the perimeter of your garden with carefully separated weeds can act like a moat, drawing in aphids, flies, and malicious worm species. It also may help you have a bit more sympathy for weeds, as you'll spend the season watching them get eaten to save your garden!

Benefit #3: Weeds Can Help Provide Nutrients

Weeds can also be used to attract helpful microorganisms including worms, which can be instrumental in breaking down organic matter.

As these organisms feed on the seeds and nectar provided by these weeds, they'll be able to further assist the vegetables you have in your primary green space. The weeds themselves can even be turned into food for your plants, becoming humus as they decay. In addition, the root systems of dead weeds can be used as tunnels for good worms to gain access to your soil.

Benefit #4: You Can Slow Erosion with the Right Weeds

If the weeds infesting your garden have large root systems, they can help you fight soil erosion. Roots will hold the soil in place, binding it to the nearby land and making it more resistant to environmental damage. This damage usually comes in the form of heavy rain or wind, which can uproot plants if the storm system is strong enough. While some weeds may not be ideal, as the disadvantages could outweigh the advantages, there are several species that can work perfectly for erosion control. Some of these species include clover, rye, vetch, rye grass, alfalfa, and barley.

Benefit #5: Some Weeds Have Culinary or Medicinal Uses

It's important to remember that weeds are just plants. Sure, they are plants you don't want, but they're plants all the same. Just like the vegetables or herbs you intentionally plant in your garden, weeds can be very useful. Here are some plants with culinary or even medicinal benefits you may want to save. (Note: The medicinal benefits of these plants have not been confirmed with long-term studies. This book is in no way intended to be a source of medical advice. It's always better to seek the help of a medical professional.)

- **Dandelion:** You've probably seen thousands of dandelions in your lifetime; as one of the most common weeds, their small yellow flowers dot the backyards of many amateur gardeners. Yes, these plants can be invasive, but that doesn't mean they should just be thrown away. Dandelions have several purported uses: they are believed to boost liver health, balance hormones, and perhaps most interestingly, their roots can even serve as a coffee substitute. Dandelions can be consumed in many ways, including in a tincture, in tea, or eaten straight from the ground.

- **Common Purslane:** Common Purslane tastes and feels similar to spinach, making it a good substitute if you need to add greens to a meal. It's high in omega-3s, which are key to cellular construction and maintenance. It also has a high level of pectin, a thickening agent used in soups, vegan chocolates, and all manner of stews.

- **Chickweed:** This small, white-tipped weed can be a hassle when it's unwanted, but its medical benefits could be incredibly helpful. Chickweed has been used to help ease stomach issues, treating constipation and other problems of the digestive tract. It is also high in vitamin C, and like dandelion, can be eaten fresh.

- **Plantain:** Plantains, whether they are *Plantago lanceolata* or *Plantago major*, have a couple of medicinal uses. Their seeds are rich in vitamins and can be consumed raw, while their leaves are anti-inflammatory and anti-microbial. You can also crush up the leaves into a powder or paste that can be applied to cuts and bruises, as well as to insect bites. This may speed up the healing process and help soothe any associated pain.

- **Ground Ivy:** Also known as creeping Charlie (everyone's least favorite Disney character), ground ivy can aid with a diverse array of ailments. It has anti-inflammatory properties, contains high levels of vitamin C, and can draw moisture out of wounds. While the plant doesn't taste very good, you can brew it into a tea and mix it with honey to cover the flavor.

- **Wood Sorrel:** Wood sorrel is best used for its juice, which has a variety of medical applications. Wood sorrel juice can help with nausea and poor appetite, treat ulcers in the mouth, and treat sore muscles when mixed with warm water. Be careful though: wood sorrel juice has a great flavor, but is very high in oxalic acid. Too much juice and you'll have issues absorbing calcium.

- **Cleavers:** Sometimes called bedstraw or goosegrass, cleavers can be made into a tea to help treat UTIs (urinary tract infections) and cleanse your kidneys. You can usually find cleaver seeds stuck to your clothes after gardening, as they are adept at adhering to many kinds of fabric.

- **Lambsquarter:** By taking the leaves of lambsquarter and grinding it into a paste, you can apply it to all kinds of injuries. Whether it be a minor scrape, insect bite, sunburn, or plain old inflammation, lambsquarters has been said to have great healing properties.

Weeds That Can Be Used as Companion Plants

We've dove into some species a bit more deeply, but there are so many weeds that can actually help your main plants thrive or provide nutritional benefits. Once you've planned what seeds you will place within the rows of your garden, study which weeds commonly grow in your area to see if they are helpful in companion planting. Any plant on the following list (and many more) could be helpful to the types of vegetables you want to grow.

- Elderflower
- Plantain
- Common mallow
- Chickweed
- Chicory
- Curly dock
- Daisy
- Dandelion
- Garlic mustard
- Red clover
- Stinging nettle
- Wild garlic
- Lambsquarter
- Milkweeds
- Wood sorrel
- Amaranthus
- Field pennycress
- Mugwort
- American Pennyroyal
- Gill-over-ground
- Heal-all
- Mullein
- Mustards
- Kang kong
- Aster
- Black-eyed Susan
- Coltsfoot
- Tickseed
- Fleabanes
- Goldenrod
- Toadflax
- Wild lettuces
- Wild sweet William
- Wormwood
- Yarrow
- Ox-eye daisy
- Purple Coneflower
- Queen Ann's lace
- Sunflower
- Tansy

Finding The Perfect Partner for Your Plants

Now that we've covered the basics, let's talk about which types of plants work best together. Choosing the pairs and partners that will be growing in close proximity is one of the most important steps in companion planting. With the right combinations, you can get the maximum benefit out of each herb, vegetable, and flower you place within your green space. Choosing incorrectly, on the other hand, could result in wasted water, sunlight, and time. In our next chapter, I will provide a guide for the best crops to pair together, and what you can do to optimize your companion planting process.

Chapter 8

Playing the Matchmaker: Plant Pairings Made in Heaven, the Best Plant Friends, and Other Helpful Tips for Companion Planting

When I first started gardening, I didn't really think about how my plants would interact with each other. I was more concerned with the final product, which vegetables I wanted to harvest and eat. Once I started to consider the plants themselves and what works best for them, I ended up stumbling onto a huge milestone revelation in my gardening career: the right companion combinations don't only benefit your plants, they benefit you as well. Finding the perfect mate for the various inhabitants of your garden leads to improved growth, healthier crops, and a higher final yield. Essentially, that original goal I had of creating edible vegetables was actually hindered by my initial tunnel vision: by focusing on the final product, I was ignoring some simple steps that could actually enhance my garden's production. I discovered this almost entirely by accident by putting two companion plants close together, basil and tomato.

There was one season where I was having a lot of trouble with my tomatoes. It seemed like they were constantly being attacked by thrips, flies, and mosquitoes. Try as I might, I could not stop the infestations that continually attacked my budding tomato plants. I continued tending to them throughout the season, even getting a somewhat decent harvest from that section of my garden. Unfortunately, the tomatoes that were produced were downright awful. They were deflated, lacking in flavor, and never quite achieved that bright red hue you associate with a healthy, plump tomato. Instead of trying to fix the problem, I just assumed it was an off-season, and put the bad tomatoes to the back of my mind. I wrote down the lackluster result in my journal, but by the next season I had basically forgotten. I planted my tomatoes in the same spot, taking no extra care to prevent any pests. But as luck would have it, I squeezed some basil in the same patch as the tomatoes. It was well into the season before I leafed through my journal, finding my note about pests and poor flavor. But to my surprise, my tomatoes were flourishing.

I didn't know at the time, but basil is one of the best companion plants for tomatoes. It repels many of the pests I was dealing with the previous season, particularly the thrips, flies, and mosquitoes. My tomatoes also seemed much more full, vibrant, and flavorful once harvested. Not only that, but the overall yield from my tomato section was off the charts. I looked around online, and found that other gardeners had similar results when planting basil with their tomatoes. The basil itself also flourished, due in part to the bit of shade tomatoes can offer during the harsh sunlight of summer.

It may seem a bit unscientific, but that's sort of how companion planting works. Many of the plant combinations we know about now were stumbled onto by accident, and while I certainly wasn't the first person to "discover" the tomato and basil pairing, I definitely won't be the last. Experimentation is important with this gardening technique, as is diligent note taking. Who knows, you may even add to the list below and help other gardeners find a new plant pairing to help their greenery thrive!

Companion Plants: Their Friends, Enemies, and Beneficial Weeds

Below I have listed some companion plants I have personally placed in my soil along with some friends and enemies I've seen help, or hinder, their growth. I've also included some beneficial weeds; if you see these species near your plants, you may actually notice that they enhance your garden's growth. It's always good to be careful with weeds though; these species can be invasive, and in some cases grow quickly. Try to find a balance and see what works best for your unique green space, and take notes as to what combinations produce the best synergistic effect.

Now, these are only the companion plants I've seen work in my own garden. There are dozens more combinations you could find that work well, so it's good to play around with the formula a bit. You also may find that, for your soil type or climate, some combinations don't work as well as others. Tinker with your garden between seasons, changing up your plant pairings and seeing the best ways to maximize your growth.

Companion Plant Master Table

Plant Type	Friends	Enemies	Beneficial Weeds
Eggplant	◗ Peppers ◗ Potatoes ◗ Spinach	◗ Fennel ◗ Geraniums ◗ Tomatoes ◗ Kohlrabi ◗ Melon	◗ Dandelion ◗ Wild mustard ◗ Wild rose
Chervil	◗ Radishes ◗ Mushrooms ◗ Asparagus	◗ Plants that don't provide shade	◗ Nettle ◗ Clover ◗ Wild rose
Asparagus	◗ Nightshades (tomato, eggplant, etc.) ◗ Dill ◗ Coriander ◗ Comfrey ◗ Basil	◗ Onions ◗ Shallots ◗ Garlic ◗ Chives ◗ Leeks	◗ Wild rose ◗ Borage ◗ Marigolds
Basil	◗ Asparagus ◗ Marigolds ◗ Peppers ◗ Tomatoes ◗ Borage	◗ Fennel ◗ Cucumbers ◗ Rue ◗ Sage ◗ Thyme	◗ Boxwood ◗ Dogwood ◗ Lilac

Cilantro	◗ Potatoes ◗ Anise ◗ Legumes	◗ Tomatoes ◗ Peppers ◗ Dill ◗ Fennel ◗ Lavender	◗ Marigolds ◗ Catnip ◗ Alyssum
Beans**	◗ Cabbage ◗ Carrots ◗ Cauliflower ◗ Kale ◗ Peas	◗ Chives ◗ Strawberries ◗ Garlic ◗ Onions	◗ Marigolds ◗ Caper spurge ◗ Wild rose
Corn	◗ Mint ◗ Cucumber ◗ Marigolds ◗ Melons ◗ Borage	◗ Celery ◗ Tomatoes ◗ Broccoli ◗ Kale ◗ Brussel Sprouts	◗ Caper spurge ◗ Wild rose ◗ Marigolds
Beets	◗ Broccoli ◗ Chard ◗ Kohlrabi ◗ Bush beans ◗ Lettuce	◗ Field mustard ◗ Charlock ◗ Pole beans	◗ Wild rose ◗ Clover ◗ Marigolds
Borage	◗ Squash ◗ Strawberries ◗ Tomatoes ◗ Cabbage ◗ Marigolds	◗ None that I know of	◗ Borage is typically considered a weed, but works well with legumes, tomatoes, and brassicas

Onions	🜄 Brassicas* 🜄 Beets 🜄 Lettuce 🜄 Chamomile	🜄 Sage 🜄 Asparagus 🜄 Peas 🜄 Beans 🜄 Other onions (if you have an issue with onion maggots)	🜄 Dandelions 🜄 Clover
Peas	🜄 Corn 🜄 Cucumber 🜄 Turnip 🜄 Mint	🜄 Chives 🜄 Garlic 🜄 Onions 🜄 Leeks 🜄 Scallions	🜄 Caper spurge 🜄 Bashful mimosa 🜄 Dandelion
Peppers	🜄 Eggplant 🜄 Cucumbers 🜄 Carrots 🜄 Squash 🜄 Radishes	🜄 Broccoli 🜄 Cauliflower 🜄 Cabbage 🜄 Brussel Sprouts 🜄 Fennel	🜄 Bashful Mimosa 🜄 Crow garlic 🜄 Caper spurge
Potatoes	🜄 Chives 🜄 Cilantro 🜄 Horseradish 🜄 Corn 🜄 Leeks	🜄 Asparagus 🜄 Pumpkin 🜄 Raspberry 🜄 Cucumber 🜄 Tomato	🜄 Crow garlic 🜄 Caper spurge 🜄 Bashful Mimosa
Radishes	🜄 Chervil 🜄 Brassicas* 🜄 Parsnip 🜄 Dill 🜄 Mint	🜄 Potatoes 🜄 Agastache 🜄 Corn 🜄 Sunflowers 🜄 Kohlrabi	🜄 Wild mustard 🜄 Marigolds 🜄 Wild dill

Spinach	◖ Cauliflower ◖ Chard ◖ Onion ◖ Peas ◖ Strawberries	◖ Potatoes ◖ Fennel ◖ Pumpkins ◖ Melons ◖ Corn	◖ Wild basil ◖ Wild mint
Tomatoes	◖ Borage ◖ Garlic ◖ Basil ◖ Parsley ◖ Asparagus	◖ Kohlrabi ◖ Broccoli ◖ Cabbage ◖ Cauliflower ◖ Rutabaga	◖ Bashful mimosa ◖ Crow garlic
Pumpkins	◖ Radish ◖ Corn ◖ Oregano ◖ Chives ◖ Chamomile	◖ Kale ◖ Brussels sprouts ◖ Cauliflower ◖ Potatoes ◖ Kohlrabi	◖ Crow garlic ◖ Wild mint ◖ Foxglove
Zucchini / Summer squash	◖ Dill ◖ Garlic ◖ Marigolds ◖ Mint ◖ Oregano	◖ Potatoes ◖ Winter squashes ◖ Melons ◖ Pumpkins ◖ Cucumbers	◖ Crow garlic ◖ Wild mint ◖ Foxglove
Cucumbers	◖ Legumes ◖ Marigolds ◖ Sunflowers ◖ Corn ◖ Dill	◖ Melon ◖ Potatoes ◖ Sage ◖ Basil ◖ Mints	◖ Nasturtiums ◖ Marigolds ◖ Crow garlic

Garden Peas	🌢 Celery 🌢 Corn 🌢 Cucumbers 🌢 Peppers 🌢 Carrots	🌢 Shallots 🌢 Leeks 🌢 Onions 🌢 Garlic 🌢 Gladioli	🌢 Crow garlic 🌢 Wild rosemary 🌢 Wild lavender
Garlic	🌢 Spinach 🌢 Strawberries 🌢 Chamomile 🌢 Peppers 🌢 Cabbage	🌢 Beans 🌢 Sage 🌢 Parsley 🌢 Peas 🌢 Asparagus	🌢 Wild mustard 🌢 Dandelions 🌢 Marigolds
Kale	🌢 Peas 🌢 Onions 🌢 Celery 🌢 Artichokes 🌢 Beets	🌢 Broccoli 🌢 Cauliflower 🌢 Swiss Chard 🌢 Brussels sprouts 🌢 Kohlrabi	🌢 Clover 🌢 Nettle 🌢 Wild mustard
Leeks	🌢 Lettuce 🌢 Beets 🌢 Cabbage 🌢 Tomatoes	🌢 Spinach 🌢 Carrots 🌢 Celery	🌢 Wild Lavender 🌢 Wild mint 🌢 Marigolds
Lettuce	🌢 Chives 🌢 Beets 🌢 Carrots 🌢 Chervil 🌢 Eggplant	🌢 Brussels sprouts 🌢 Rutabaga 🌢 Turnip 🌢 Cabbage 🌢 Broccoli	🌢 Marigolds 🌢 Wild mustard 🌢 Wild rose

Mustard	🌢 Corn 🌢 Dill 🌢 Garlic 🌢 Celery 🌢 Mint	🌢 Soybeans 🌢 Sunflower 🌢 Strawberries 🌢 Beans 🌢 Shepherd's purse	🌢 Marigolds 🌢 Crow garlic 🌢 Nettle
Broccoli	🌢 Other brassicas* 🌢 Oregano 🌢 Rosemary 🌢 Shallots 🌢 Rhubarb	🌢 Corn 🌢 Tomatoes 🌢 Peppers 🌢 Cucurbits 🌢 Strawberries	🌢 Nettle 🌢 Wild mustard 🌢 Clover

*Full List of Brassicas:

🌢 Bok Choy
🌢 Collard
🌢 Kale
🌢 Kohlrabi
🌢 Napa Cabbage

🌢 Brown Mustard
🌢 Broccoli
🌢 Brussels Sprouts
🌢 Cabbage

🌢 Napus
🌢 Rutabaga
🌢 Turnip
🌢 Cauliflower

**Pole Beans and Bush Beans

Best in Show: The Beneficial Weed Awards

You'll see a couple of weeds showing up several times in that list, with borage getting its own space on the table. I think that many weed species get a bad rap (refer to Chapter 7 for a fuller explanation) and I wanted to take the time to highlight some of their benefits. So I've selected three species of plants we commonly think of as weeds to shine a bit of light on their benefits.

The Best Pest Control Award Goes to… Marigolds!

Pest Control Advantages of Marigolds

Root-Knot Nematode: Root-knot nematodes are notoriously hard to deal with, and an infestation of these bad bugs can spell disaster for your garden. A type of roundworm, root-knot nematodes will feed on root cells with needle-like parts of their mouth (known as stylets). Luckily, the marigold has your back. The roots of the marigold plant secrete a chemical known as alpha-terthienyl, which can slow or stop the development of nematode eggs.

Whiteflies: French marigolds, or *Tagetes Patula,* are specifically effective against whiteflies. This harmful insect will suck the juice out of your leaves, causing them to yellow and grow more slowly. With a big enough infestation, your plants will wither and die. Whiteflies hate the limonene present in marigolds, and will flee at the first sign of this chemical compound. These work best as a precautionary measure though, as planting marigolds into your garden after your plants are already infested won't do nearly as much.

Slugs and Snails: While it would be great if marigolds also drove away slugs and snails, they actually do the opposite. Marigolds will draw in both types of slimy garden critters, causing them to feed on its leaves and stems. This can be just as helpful as serving as a repellent; your marigolds can serve as decoys to distract slugs and snails from moving on to your more important plants. Creating a protective barrier of marigolds around your garden gives these creatures an easier food source so they don't need to push further into your green space.

The Best Plant for Fertilization Award Goes to... Borage!

In addition to adding a beautiful blue hue to your greenery, borage has a number of purported medicinal benefits. Borage may be helpful with fevers, coughs, adrenal insufficiency, difficulties urinating, lung inflammation, and can serve as a sedative. In the same way borage can keep you healthy, it can also keep your garden healthy. The way it does this is by acting as a great organic fertilizer. With deep taproots, borage soaks up nutrients from deep within your soil, primarily nitrogen. These can be redistributed to the upper levels of your garden by properly preparing your borage. By soaking the leaves or smashing up the plants whole, you can create a soil-enriching material to spread on your plants.

The Best Shelter Plant Award Goes to... Wild Basil!

We talked about partial-sun or partial-shade plants, which need to be protected from direct sunlight. To provide the dappled sunlight these plants require to thrive, you need to have some way of filtering the harsh light of midday. One of the best natural ways to accomplish this is with basil. Wild basil is a full-sun plant, thriving in direct sunlight and warm conditions. It can also be very dense, and grow as high as six inches tall. This makes it perfect to shield seedlings or lower-lying plants, especially if they need a bit more humidity or shade.

Twenty Tips to Make Your Companion Plants Thrive

Tip #1: Don't Skimp on the Herbs and Flowers

Herbs and flowers can help increase the flower production and overall yield of your garden. By attracting beneficial insects (which help protect your vegetables), raising the levels of nectar production, and bringing in valuable pollinators, you'll end up with much more to harvest once your vegetables are ripe.

Tip #2: Be Mindful of The Space Between Your Plants

Make sure to research how much room your individual plants need, both from each other and from structures near your garden. This distance can range from a few inches to several feet, depending on the species and obstruction you are making space from.

Tip #3: Plant Fast-Growing Plants Near Slow-Growing Ones to Maximize Your Production

You can maximize space by planting fast-growing plants in between and around slower-growing ones. This also helps increase the overall yield of your garden; by having varied harvest times, you can raise the total level of production your green space is capable of. A good example of this is planting lettuce and radishes with melon and squash. The lettuce and radishes will grow quickly, even allowing you to harvest multiple times from a single crop. The melons and squash will grow slower, and by the time their vines need more space, you'll have already harvested your faster-growing crops.

Tip #4: Use Corn as a Natural Light Filter

If you have plants that prefer partial shade or partial sun, corn can be a great way to naturally filter light during the harsh direct sunlight of midday. Plants like spinach, Swiss chard, and bush beans all thrive under the shade provided by corn stalks. They also work well in close proximity as they don't compete for water or nutrients. While corn isn't technically your only option, and there are structures you can build to get this "dappled sunlight" artificially, it's always better to do so organically. You can also harvest the corn afterwards, adding to the overall yield of your garden.

Tip #5: Plant Beans and Corn with Lettuce at Their Bases

Similar to the Three Sisters method, where Native Americans would plant corn, beans, and squash together (refer to Chapter 1 to see a more in-depth description of this), there is a similar synchronicity if you swap squash for lettuce. Lettuce, as a crop that doesn't require too much direct sunlight, benefits from the shade provided by the corn and bean plants.

Tip #6: Marigolds Can Serve as a Great Rabbit Distraction

One common misconception I've run into is that marigolds are a great way to deter rabbits from eating your plants. While marigolds are certainly effective at turning away root-knot nematodes and whiteflies, they will do nothing to stop an infestation of rabbits. Luckily, you can use this to your advantage! Plant marigolds around the perimeter or in a separate patch from your main plants to draw rabbits away. Instead of munching on your crops, they will chow down on these marigolds and leave your primary garden alone.

Tip #7: Dill Will Bring in the Wasps, Which Can Kill Cabbage Worms

In addition to being a delicious and useful herb, dill will also attract a number of beneficial insects into your green space. Dill is known to attract green lacewings, ladybugs, tachinid flies, hoverflies, mealybug destroyers, and aphid midges. If you have cabbage, dill could be the best way to deal with their natural enemy, the cabbage worm. By attracting braconid wasps, dill will help eradicate this devastating pest and keep your cabbages growing strong.

Tip #8: Radishes Love Squash and Cucumbers

Radishes are a great companion for a huge variety of plants, including beans, beets, chervil, celeriac, lettuce, mint, peas, parsnip, spinach, and tomatoes. They are particularly good to plant near squash and cucumbers, due to the pests that tend to ravage these types of crops. Radishes are adept at repelling cucumber beetles along with other squash-family pests, helping keep your cucumbers and squash safe.

Tip #9: Garlic and Chives Can Repel Aphids from Your Rose Bushes

Pests absolutely love chowing down on the sweet flavor of rose bushes, with aphids being a particularly pervasive pest for this type of plant. Fortunately, garlic and chives can help save your roses by emitting strong smells from their heavily scented leaves and stems. Not only will they drive away aphids, but you can eat the garlic and chives come harvest time!

Tip #10: Beans and Potatoes Balance Each Other's Nitrogen Levels

Keeping the appropriate levels of nitrogen is important for many plants; beans and potatoes are no different. Planting these two in close proximity can help strike an appropriate nitrogen balance, with beans adding the nitrogen potatoes crave. Beans can also help deter certain types of pests; for example, green beans can drive away potato beetles while continuing to add nitrogen to the soil.

Tip #11: Squash Can Help with Weeds

Through the use of allelochemicals, squash plants can help inhibit the growth of highly competitive species. During rainy periods or regular watering times, these allelochemicals are pulled from the squashes' leaves and drip down into the soil. These chemicals tend only to affect invasive species, leaving your other crops alone in their weed-killing pursuit. Squash is also a plant that can provide a lot of shade, which can block the sun from patches of soil and further hinder weed growth.

Tip #12: Flowers Can Protect Your Vegetables

Flowers are a good way to protect and enhance the growth of your plants for several reasons. They can attract beneficial bugs like ladybugs or pollinators like bees, helping ward off pests and pollinate your plants. They can also serve as distractions for bad bugs to munch on, leaving your main crop to grow in peace.

Tip #13: Avoid Planting Members of the Same Family Too Close Together

While this isn't a hard and fast rule, planting members of the same family close together can sometimes lead to complications. Having a large number of similar plants in close proximity can attract larger numbers of common pests, encourage outbreaks of family-specific diseases, and cause competition for nutrients. It's always better to mix it up, keeping those that attract similar pests separated and rotating crops that tend to provide or consume the same nutrient.

Tip #14: Intersperse Herbs and Flowers Together

Mixing herbs and flowers in your garden has several distinct benefits. Both can act as trap crops, serving as a sacrifice to the pest gods by attracting pests that would otherwise eat up your viable crops. They can also attract pollinators, primarily bees; herbs in the mint family like oregano and thyme are particularly adept at this. Herbs and flowers can also bring in other beneficial insects like lacewings, parasitic wasps, ground beetles, and ladybugs. In addition to all this, they can repel harmful insects like moths, worms, beetles, aphids, and flies.

Tip #15: Radishes Are Great with Other Brassicas

Although I previously advised to avoid planting brassicas close to other members of the same family, radishes and certain other brassicas work quite well together, with plants like kale, spinach, and broccoli helping to enrich the soil with the nutrients radishes need. Radishes can also help suppress weeds, act as a trap crop, and help break up soil that is suffering from high levels of compaction.

Tip #16: Document Your Companion Garden Carefully

Like with any garden venture, keeping a detailed and comprehensive journal about your green space is essential to future success. By documenting your companion garden, you can see what types of plants tend to do well near one another, what sunlight and water levels create the most conducive growing environment, and what small tweaks you can make to encourage your plants to thrive.

Tip #17: Tall Plants Can Protect Companions Prone to Bolting

Bolting is a process that occurs when plants set seed too early, and can often curb the harvest of a crop. Plants do this as a sort of survival mechanism: when put under large amounts of stress, plants will bolt so they can quickly produce seed to start the next generation. The unfortunate result is that you will have fewer tasty vegetables. One major stressor is too much direct sunlight; a great way to avoid this is by planting tall, shady plants near your more vulnerable garden residents. That way they can filter the sunlight and protect those plants during the harsh light of midday. Plants that are particularly prone to bolting include arugula, spinach, lettuces and coriander.

Tip #18: Try Intercropping

In the simplest terms, intercropping is planting two or more crops very close to one another, in the same row, strip, or bed. This allows them to interact, and is the basis for most companion planting. There are a number of different intercropping methods. These can include:

- **Relay Cropping:** Planting a second crop in the same field before the first crop is harvested.

- **Interseeding:** Planting two crops together. These can be planted at the same time, or the second can be planted after the first is established.

- **Overseeding:** Planting a second plant or a cover crop into an already established garden. This is usually done by scattering seeds on top of the soil without covering them with dirt. This is known as Surface Sowing.

- **Polycultures:** Having multiple interacting plants in one space.

- **Smother Cropping:** A cover crop interseeded with the intention of smothering weeds.

- **Live Mulch:** Planting permanent strips of grass between rows.

Mix and match these methods to see what works best for your garden, and find the techniques that function the most effectively for your climate, plant type, and available space.

Tip #19: Be Careful with Fast-Growing Companion Plants like Mint

Many of your plants will grow at different speeds, with slower plants like squash and melons taking their sweet time getting to the right size, and other plants like cilantro and basil growing at incredible speeds. One of the fastest-growing plants is mint, which can quickly become an invasive species if not monitored. Their roots are known as "runners" and will spread and create new plants at a rapid pace. If you don't keep them sequestered in their own area, mint can overtake your other companion plants and eventually your entire garden.

I honestly feel that mint should come with a warning label: "Caution: invasive species that makes kudzu seem difficult to grow!"

Tip #20: Don't Forget to Have Fun!

While some people may think gardening is all business, it doesn't have to be. Make sure to find ways to make gardening fun instead of a chore. If you are having a good time, you are more likely to keep your green space well maintained and research further techniques to help it thrive.

Once my gardens are up and running for the year, I tend to do as much daily maintenance as I can first thing in the morning before the heat of the day sets in. I make it fun by enjoying the silly things in life such as watering my garden at 7:00 am while wearing my pajamas and waving at my neighbors as they drink their morning coffee on their front porch.

Companion Planting is Your Best Bet for Getting the Most Out of Your Garden

We've covered just about everything we can about companion planting, from the proper way to maintain and care for your plants and which insects will affect your greenspace, to the best and worst combinations of crops you could put in your garden. With the volume of information we've covered, it's understandable to not remember every little detail. As we close out the book, let's take a look back at the key points covered in each chapter, and review a couple of details that can help ensure your companion garden is a roaring success.

COMMUNITY IS KEY

Help Yourself

I hope you have enjoyed reading this book as much as I have enjoyed writing it. I also hope that this book has helped you and that your garden will thrive with the tips I have offered. The last bit of advice I can give you is that you need to join a community. Having an unlimited source of help from gardeners who have been there and done that will help you more than you can imagine. Whenever you have a question, a good community will offer advice that they have gained from experience. Something that is brand new to you will most likely be something that someone else has already encountered, and they will be happy to give you the answer you need. There are many great gardening communities all over the world. Find one (or several) that you like and join them.

To further help gardeners like you and me, I have created such a community on Facebook. I would love for you to join us! You can find "Soil Basics for Vegetable Gardening" by going to facebook.com/groups/soilbasics.

A gardening community is essential to success. Trying to go at it alone can lead to years of frustration or to giving up before you ever have a truly successful garden. It is through the kindness of others who are willing to offer help to someone they don't even know that a gardening community grows, knowledge is shared, and gardens thrive!

Help Others

So now I ask you this, would you help a struggling gardener you've never met if it only took a second or two of your time and it didn't cost you anything? If you answered yes, I would like to offer you the opportunity to help a stranger right now. While one shouldn't judge a book by its cover, you know as well as I do that most folks do. They also judge a book by its reviews! The more positive reviews a book has, the more likely a person is to buy it. So, for me and for others, please take a second to leave this book a review on Amazon. The more reviews this book has, the more likely it will be that others will be helped by the information contained. It only takes a second.

Conclusion

Whether it's enlisting the help of another person or the help of another plant, it never hurts to work together. Companion planting isn't just a way to help you get more out of your plants; it's a way for them to get more out of each other. Nature is a series of natural balances, and we as humans sometimes forget that. In natural ecosystems, many species coexist and thrive together in perfect harmony, and by bringing that principle into your greenspace, you can benefit from the natural rhythms that have helped plants thrive for millions of years.

Now, I understand we covered a lot of topics in this book, and I don't expect you to memorize everything. I've taken the time to review and break down each chapter in an effort to make finding the information you need a bit easier. Whenever you have a question or want to find a certain piece of info, you can refer to this list to save a bit of time.

Here is a brief look back at what we've learned.

Chapter 1: *Greenery Loves Company: A Closer Look at Companion Planting*

In this chapter, we took a deep dive into the history of companion planting, starting with the Native American technique known as "The Three Sisters." From these humble origins, companion planting grew and changed throughout history, with different countries and societies adding to our knowledge of beneficial plant pairings.

We also covered the mechanisms by which companion planting functions, starting with identifying the beneficial characteristics of different plant species. These benefits include:

- Erosion protection
- Moisture retention
- Weed suppression
- Pest control

- Disease resilience
- Beneficial bug attraction
- Providing shade

Chapter 2: *Sow Wrong: Common Mistakes to Weed Out from Your System*

This chapter covers the basic mistakes most gardeners make during their first few seasons. These problems include:

- Planting too early or too late
- Neglecting to harvest
- Picking the wrong spot
- Not spacing properly
- Skimping on your soil
- Planting too much
- Forgetting to stagger harvest times
- Putting off routine maintenance
- Planting without a fence
- Ignoring the signs of poor health

We then talked about the common problems that many face when they begin companion planting specifically, including neglecting to give companion plants enough space to grow, making sure that your plants don't block too much sunlight, and paying special attention to the size and depth of roots. Incompatible plants are also discussed in this chapter, though this subject is covered in more detail in Chapter 8.

Chapter 3: *Seeds for Growth: How to Get Started with Companion Planting*

Chapter 3 is dedicated to discussing the different stages of planning your companion garden and the factors that will affect your success. These include:

- Choosing a specific gardening goal
- Creating a space that you can manage,
- Considering the type of climate you are planting in
- Keeping a journal to track your progress

We also talked about the different types of companion planting layouts you can use, focusing on several key types to show their strengths and weaknesses. These types include:

- Traditional row
- Square-foot layout
- Perennial polyculture
- Mandala garden
- Keyhole bed
- Organic form

Chapter 4: *Digging Deeper: It's Soil That Matters*

The foundation for any successful garden is soil, so this chapter focused mainly on the different components that make up the best base for your garden. We covered the characteristics of healthy soil, primarily how rich it is in organic matter, whether it has the right texture, and whether it has a good pH balance.

We then talked about some soil tests you can conduct to help determine if you need to make adjustments, as well as how you can change your soil's pH. Then, we covered the necessity of avoiding soil compaction and disruption, along with the importance of organic matter. The most important kind of organic matter you'll have in your garden is compost, which is why I reserved a healthy chunk of this chapter to describe how you can make your own compost at home.

Chapter 5: *Let There be Light... and Water*

Chapter 5 is all about garden maintenance, and how the combination of light and water are key for healthy companion plant growth. We covered the different types of sunlight intensity plants thrive within, namely:

- Full sun
- Partial sun
- Partial shade
- Full shade

We also looked at how you can measure the sunlight your garden regularly gets.

Then, we talked about watering: how to stick to a regular schedule, how much water to utilize, and how to save water whenever possible. Part of this is the utilization of mulch, which not only gives your plants vital nutrients but also helps retain moisture and deliver it to the areas your plants need it most.

Chapter 6: *The Good, the Bad, and the Ugly: Using Companion Planting to Naturally Drive Away Harmful Bugs and Attract Beneficial Ones*

Insects are as much a part of your garden as your plants are, and discerning the beneficial from the harmful is a huge part of keeping your green space healthy. Chapter 6 covers the role of insects in detail, categorizing bugs into the "good" and "bad".

Good bugs tend to fall into three categories:

◗ Pollinators

◗ Predators

◗ Parasites

Each has a distinct role and set of advantages they can offer to your greenery. I made sure to go into a number of examples that fall into each category so you know what to look for. This chapter also showed you which companion plants will help you bring in these bugs (though there is a table in Chapter 1 that can help you as well.)

I also covered a number of harmful insects, and talked about the kind of damage they can do to your companion plants. There is also a list of plants in this chapter that will help you repel these bad bugs, ranging from basil and onion to tomatoes and catnip.

Chapter 7: *Weeding Between the Lines: Understanding the Role of Weeds in Your Garden*

Weeds are the most condemned and hated plants you'll find in the gardening world, but they don't have to be. In this chapter, we discussed some facts everyone should know about weeds, including the fact that a weed is technically just a plant "growing in the wrong place."

We also talk about some beneficial effects you may not know about, and weeds that can be used as companion plants. You may recognize some of these weeds from your garden, and will be surprised to know that they may actually help your plants instead of hurt them!

Chapter 8: *Playing the Matchmaker: Plant Pairings Made in Heaven, the Best Plant Friends, and Other Helpful Tips for Companion Planting*

For the final chapter, we dove deep into the plant pairings that I have personally utilized over the years, including looking at a table I created that shows each plant's friends, enemies, and beneficial weeds. We also highlighted some lesser-known companion plants, specifically marigolds, borage, and basil. Each of these can give your garden a distinct growing edge that could drastically increase your yield. The chapter concludes with a list of tips to help your companion garden thrive, which covers everything from ways to boost nutrient availability to optimal combinations of different plant species.

What I Hope You Take Away

My goal by writing this second book was to help provide the guidelines you'll need to successfully companion plant. By learning the basics of soil, good garden maintenance, and the right combinations of plants to place together, you'll be able to plant a better garden than you ever thought imaginable. I also hope you use the knowledge I've provided here as a foundation on which to build; as you become more experienced, you will start to find your own tips and tricks to use. This will make each growing season a little better than the last, until you find that your garden flourishes year after year.

If you enjoyed this book, it would mean a lot to me if you left a review on Amazon. I think that the level of research and time put into these pages can really benefit amateur gardeners, and I want as many people as possible to have the information they need. Good gardening can change lives, and I truly believe that everyone has the ability to create lush and productive green space that they can be proud of.

Companion planting is an ever-growing and ever-changing gardening technique. At the beginning of the book, we talked about the various people throughout history who have added to these methods, and how each of their contributions helped other gardeners down the line. Keep putting in the time and taking diligent notes and who knows, your name could be added to this list as one of the great contributors to the field of companion planting!

Don't forget to get your FREE GIFT!

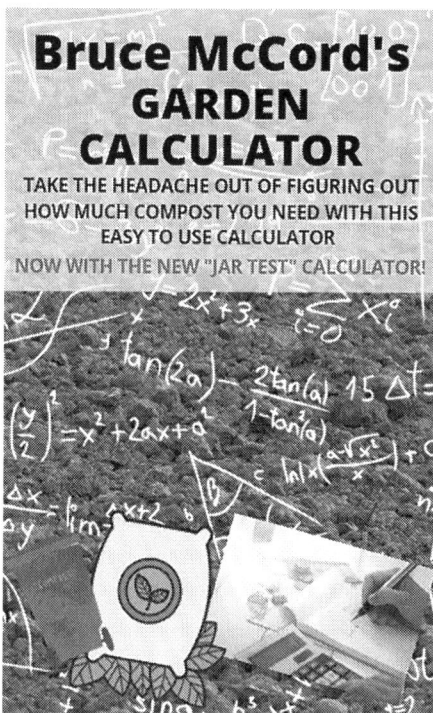

With Bruce McCord's Garden Calculator you will...

- Save time and avoid headaches!

- Save money by avoiding miscalculations

- Easily determine how much compost you need for your garden

- Find out in seconds how many bags, yards, or scoops you need

- Use the same calculator for mulch, topsoil, gravel, virtually ANYTHING

- There's a Metric option too!

Get your FREE COPY today by visiting:
www.BruceMcCord.com

Acknowledgments

Once again, I must start by thanking my amazing wife, Amanda. I can honestly say that none of my books would exist without her continuing support.

I would like to give a huge thank you to my content checking team Stephanie, Toni, Charles, and Emmett.

About the Author

Bruce McCord is a passionate gardener and the author of *Basic Soil Science for Successful Vegetable Gardening* and *Basic Companion Planting for Successful Vegetable Gardening*.

Through years of research and testing the science on his own garden, Bruce has developed a sharp understanding of the difference that soil composition makes to the productivity and health of a garden. Determined to make this information more accessible to the everyday gardener, he focused his writing on making soil science relatable to beginners. He has now expanded that focus to include companion planting.

Bruce has always been a keen gardener, beginning his journey on his grandmother's vegetable plot as a child. As he got older and began to work on his own land, he realized that the magic his grandmother created had much more science behind it than he'd ever understood. He turned his attention to soil science, reading and researching everything he could get his hands on and applying the theory to his vegetable patch. Through years of trial and error and extensive reading, he has come to understand the winning formula for a flourishing garden.

Bruce works in aircraft maintenance, and gardening has always been his way to relax and escape from the worries of daily life. He remembers his early gardening attempts and the frustrations that came with them and is determined to help other gardeners sidestep that frustration so they can benefit from the relaxing and healing qualities of gardening.

Bruce has been married for 16 years, and he and his wife love spending time together in their garden. They have a passion for rescuing blind diabetic dogs and share their lives with a small pack of special animals. He also enjoys the theater and has a particular love of Broadway musicals.

Reference

🌢 *10 Biggest Vegetable Gardening Mistakes We've All Made. (2022, February 9). The Spruce.* https://www.thespruce.com/ biggest-vegetable-gardening-mistakes-1402993

🌢 *10 Incredible Facts About Dirt. (2016, April 13). Audubon.* https:// www.audubon.org/news/10-incredible-facts-about-dirt

🌢 AFBFA - American Farm Bureau Foundation for Agriculture. (2022). *The Three Sisters. AFBFA 2022.* https://www. agfoundation.org/news/the-three-sisters

🌢 Andrychowicz, A. (2022, May 17). *A Beginner's Guide To Companion Planting. Get Busy Gardening.* https:// getbusygardening.com/companion-planting/

🌢 Andrychowicz, A. (2022b, July 5). *How Much Sunlight Does My Garden Get – The Ultimate Sun Exposure Guide. Get Busy Gardening.* https://getbusygardening.com/how-to-determine-sun-exposure/

🌢 *The Basics of Companion Planting Garden Crops. (2021, November 29). The Spruce.* https://www.thespruce.com/ companion-planting-with-chart-5025124

139

🝆 Hort Zone (2018, December 20). *12 Plants That Attract Ruthless Good Bugs. Hort Zone. https://www.hortzone.com/blog/plants-attract-ruthless-good-bugs/*

🝆 *Companion Planting Guide for Vegetables. (2022). Almanac.com.* https://www.almanac.com/companion-planting-guide-vegetables

🝆 *Companion Plants Repel Garden Pests and Attract Beneficial Insects. (2020, October 21). The Spruce.* https://www.thespruce.com/companion-planting-1402735

🝆 Cotton, L. (2013, May 31). *Companion Planting and Listening to Your Weeds. Grow Appalachia.* https://growappalachia.berea.edu/2013/05/31/companion-planting-and-listening-to-your-weeds/

🝆 Homestead and Chill (2020, March 14). *Companion Planting 101 (w/ Garden Companion Planting Chart). Homesteadandchill.com* https://homesteadandchill.com/benefits-companion-planting-chart/

🝆 Dian Farmer (2022a, May 28). *Benefits And Effects Of Weeds In Your Garden. Dian Farmer Learning To Grow Our Own Food.* https://dianfarmer.com/benefits-and-effects-of-weeds-in-your-garden/

🝆 Damerow, G. (2021, December 17). *Gardening Tips: 12 Common Gardening Mistakes to Avoid. Countryside.* https://www.iamcountryside.com/growing/gardening-tips-12-gardening-mistakes/

🝆 *Describe how weeds are categorized by life cycle and how this is. (2016, January 9). Forage Information System.* https://forages.oregonstate.edu/nfgc/eo/onlineforagecurriculum/instructormaterials/availabletopics/weeds/lifecycle

🝆 Doyle, S. (2021, April 7). *10 Most Common Garden Pests and How to Fight Them. Gardening.* https://gardening.org/10-most-common-garden-pests-and-how-to-fight-them/

🌱 Food, F. B. C. (2022, July 17). *Three Simple Ways to Test Your Soil. BC Farms & Food.* https://bcfarmsandfood.com/three-simple-ways-test-soil/

🌱 Gardening Channel (2020, June 9). *26 Vegetables That Can Grow In Partial Shade. Gardeningchannel.com* https://www.gardeningchannel.com/sun-and-shade-loving-vegetables-list/

🌱 Garden Pals (2022b, May 9). *Gardening Statistics in 2022 (incl. Covid & Millennials). Garden Pals.* https://gardenpals.com/gardening-statistics/

🌱 Green, K. (2021, March 19). *Weeds as Companion Plants. Maine Organic Farmers and Gardeners.* https://www.mofga.org/resources/weeds/weeds-as-companion-plants/

🌱 *Hazards of Yard & Garden Pesticides. (2016, December 14). Alaska Community Action On Toxics.* https://www.akaction.org/tackling_toxics/yard-garden/pesticides/

🌱 *Healthy Soil and How to Make It. (2022, June 14). The Spruce.* https://www.thespruce.com/healthy-soil-and-how-to-make-it-2539853

🌱 Hicks-Hamblin, K. (2022, May 9). *The Scientifically-Backed Benefits of Companion Planting. Gardener's Path.* https://gardenerspath.com/how-to/organic/benefits-companion-planting/

🌱 *How Many Days Can Plants Go Without Water? (2022, February 20). Gardening Mentor.* https://gardeningmentor.com/how-many-days-can-plants-go-without-water/#:%7E:text=The%20typical%20fully%2Dgrown%20plants,than%204%20to%207%20days

🌱 *How Soil Amendments Can Help Your Garden. (2019, July 8). The Spruce.* https://www.thespruce.com/soil-amendments-defined-how-to-use-2131001

🌱 *How to Test Your Garden Soil (And 3 DIY Tests). (2022). Almanac. Com.* https://www.almanac.com/content/3-simple-diy-soil-tests

🌢 *Introduction to Weeds: What are Weeds and Why do we Care? (2022, July 6). Penn State Extension.* https://extension.psu.edu/introduction-to-weeds-what-are-weeds-and-why-do-we-care

🌢 Jones, S. (2018, September 28). *The History Of Companion Planting. Growing Guides.* https://growing-guides.co.uk/the-history-of-companion-planting/

🌢 Lombardo, L. (2021, June 18). *How to Grow Your Best Garden with Companion Planting. The Self Sufficient HomeAcre.* https://www.theselfsufficienthomeacre.com/2020/02/how-to-grow-your-best-garden-with-companion-planting.html

🌢 Mel's Garden (2018, October 4). *Companion Planting Guide. Mel's Garden.* https://wheelbarrowexpert.com/companion-planting-guide/#History_of_Companion_Planting

🌢 Our Inspired Roots (2022, January 31). *Companion Planting and Plant Guilds: How to Get Started. Our Inspired Roots.* https://ourinspiredroots.com/companion-planting-and-plant-guilds-how-to-get-started/

🌢 Creative Vegetable Gardener (2022, May 30). *Secrets to Watering Your Vegetable Garden the Right Way. Creative Vegetable Gardener.* https://www.creativevegetablegardener.com/watering-vegetable-garden/#:%7E:text=In%20general%2C%20vegetable%20plants%20need,from%20rain%20and%20your%20watering

🌢 MaximumYield. (2018, November 28). *Companion Planting.* https://www.maximumyield.com/definition/763/companion-planting

🌢 M.C. (2020c, November 8). *Full Sun vs. Partial Shade: 5 Types of Sunlight for Gardening. MasterClass.* https://www.masterclass.com/articles/types-of-sunlight-for-gardening

- Miller, C. (2022, June 24). *21 Companion Plants to Consider for Pest Control. Bustling Nest.* https://bustlingnest.com/companion-plants-for-pest-control/

- Muntean, L. (2021, March 26). *How to manage garden weeds with mulch. AgriLife Today.* https://agrilifetoday.tamu.edu/2021/03/26/how-to-manage-garden-weeds-with-mulch/

- Myers, V. (2016, November 2). *Beneficial Insects You Want in Your Garden. Western Garden Centers.* https://westerngardens.com/beneficial-insects-garden/

- Patterson, S., & More, R. (2019, August 24). *Which Soil Is Best for Plant Growth? LoveToKnow.* https://garden.lovetoknow.com/wiki/Which_Soil_Is_Best_for_Plant_Growth

- Pavlis, R. (2018, July 31). *Companion Planting: Truth or Myth? Garden Myths.* https://www.gardenmyths.com/companion-planting-truth-myth/

- Pavlis, R. (2021, February 23). *Sun Mapping Your Garden the Easy Way. Garden Fundamentals.* https://www.gardenfundamentals.com/sun-mapping-garden/

- Poindexter, J. (2020, April 30). *19 Vegetable Garden Plans & Layout Ideas That Will Inspire You. MorningChores.* https://morningchores.com/vegetable-garden-plans/

- Polomski, R. F., Shaughnessy, D., & Williamson, J. (2022, May 9). *Controlling Weeds by Cultivating & Mulching | Home & Garden Information Center. Home & Garden Information Center | Clemson University, South Carolina.* https://hgic.clemson.edu/factsheet/controlling-weeds-by-cultivating-mulching/

- *Practice the good neighbor policy in the garden: Try companion. (2018, March 23). Life at OSU.* https://today.oregonstate.edu/news/practice-good-neighbor-policy-garden-try-companion-planting

- Sagouspe, T. (2021, May 19). *Sun Requirements For Plants: A Complete Guide. Rise.* https://www.buildwithrise.com/stories/demystifying-backyard-plants-sun-requirements

- Savonen, C. S. J. (2016, May 4). *Wade through truth, myth of companion plants. Statesman Journal.* https://eu.statesmanjournal.com/story/life/2016/05/04/wade-through-truth-myth-companion-plants/83835862/

- Vinje, E. (2018, November 19). *How to Improve Garden Soil Quality. Planet Natural.* https://www.planetnatural.com/organic-gardening-guru/soil/

- Vinje, E. (2018, December 27). *Lawn and Garden Chemicals. Planet Natural.* https://www.planetnatural.com/garden-chemicals/

- Waddington, E. (2021, January 11). *7 Vegetable Garden Layout Ideas To Grow More Food In Less Space. Rural Sprout.* https://www.ruralsprout.com/vegetable-garden-layout-ideas/

- Walliser, J. (2021, March 5). *14 Companion Plants to Repel Beetles and Other Garden Pests. Hobby Farms.* https://www.hobbyfarms.com/14-companion-plants-to-repel-beetles-and-other-garden-pests-3/

- Williams, S. (2019, June 15). *Ten Facts About Garden Bugs. KickassFacts.Com.* https://www.kickassfacts.com/garden-bug-facts/

- Ziton, T. (2022, July 9). *How to Choose, Plant, and Grow Companion Plants (6 Steps). Couch to Homestead.* https://couchtohomestead.com/how-to-companion-plant/

Made in the USA
Middletown, DE
08 September 2023

38218879R00094